Living in Fear on the Aryan Side

By
Halina Zawadzka

Translated by
Halina Zawadzka and Eva Baumann

EAGLE EDITIONS
2007

EAGLE EDITIONS
AN IMPRINT OF HERITAGE BOOKS, INC.

Books, CDs, and more—Worldwide

For our listing of thousands of titles see our website
at
www.HeritageBooks.com

Published 2007 by
HERITAGE BOOKS, INC.
Publishing Division
65 East Main Street
Westminster, Maryland 21157-5026

Copyright © 2004 Halina Zawadzka

Originally published in Polish under the title
Ucieczka z Getta by *Osrodek Karta*, in 2001.
Copyright by Halina Zawadzka, 2001.
Copyright by *Osrodek Karta*, 2001

International Standard Book Number: 978-0-7884-2488-2

TO MY SON ANDRZEJ
AND MY GRANDCHILDREN
ADAM AND LEA

TABLE OF CONTENTS

LIST OF PHOTOGRAPHS

1. The family Kon: mother Leonia, born Szpitbaum, father Daniel Hipolit, Halina (the author) and her brother Jerzy, summer1927.

2. Halina with her brother Jerzy in Czarniecka Gora, summer 1937.

3. ID of Daniel Hipolit Kon issued by the Germans, Konskie July 1940.

4. Halina with her half sister Helenka in Konskie, 1941.

5. Halina in Konskie,1941.

6. Karolina Slowik, Starachowice, August 1944.

7.Olga (Dziunia) Slowik, Starachowice, August 1944.

8. The titles of "The Righteous Among The Nations" issued by Yad Vashem to Karolina Slowik and her daughters Olga Dziunia) and Maria Kamer for saving Halina's life during the WWII.

POLAND

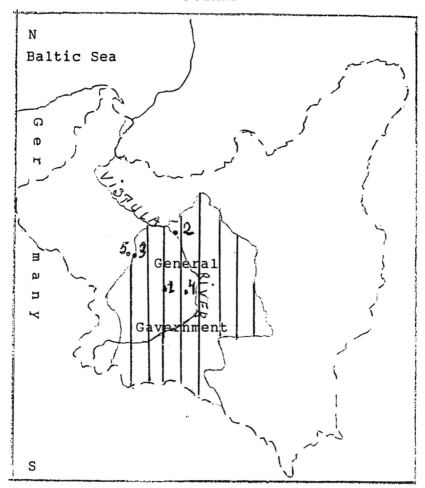

--- Polish borders before September 1939.
1.Konskie; 2.Warsaw; 3.Koluszki;
4.Starachowice; 5.Lodz.

ACKNOWLEDGMENT

I would like to acknowledge my gratitude to Eva Baumann for her productive collaboration and profound dedication to the task of translation of this book.

I would like also to express my sincere thanks to Diane and Jerry Koons, Barbara and Adam Broner, Winafred Schoeffler and Leeny Sack for their support, encouragement and invaluable help during the preparation of the manuscript.

INTRODUCTION
(BY THE PUBLISHER OF THE POLISH EDITION)

Very seldom the testimony written half a century after the events have taken place creates the impression of having been recorded immediately, moment by moment after the happenings. This is written motion and thought as if it took place only a short time ago... It reads rather like the record of a professional writer and not as a witness account.

Halina Zawadzka is a careful witness to the past. Each page of her book is like a cell of her memory - bound to the course of events and the personality of the author.

Professor Tomasz Szarota of the Warsaw University stated that this book represents a rare testimony which "has value missed in the texts written earlier". Elapsing time creates the natural selection of the remembered happenings, emotions and experiences saving only the most characteristic for the picture of the past. The people who were silent for tens of years could sometimes be more truthful about the years of German occupation than their predecessors.

Contemporary readers might have difficulties believing the improbable coincidences described in this book. I might wonder how could the author, who escaped from the Ghetto in Konskie to the surprisingly hostile "Polish world" (albeit with the exceptions contradicting the rules), avoid in such successful ways all the deadly traps of the Nazi occupation?

We do not know how many of the nine thousand Jews who were confined to the Konskie Ghetto in 1942, survived the war; certainly not many. The author thought it was a dozen or so and this number indicated the probability of her own fate. If not for all the lucky situations during her desperate flight from death we would not have this testimony today.

We do not contest the accuracy of the general historical facts described in this book, considering more important the way the author has learned about them, what was stored in her memory and its impact on her life at that time.

Reading this book is not easy for the Polish people. The picture of the Polish nation during the Second Word War described here is not in accordance with the notions about its wartime attitude toward the annihilation of the Jews.

However, the book also describes the brave Polish women in this hostile environment, who were hiding an unknown Jewish girl in their home. They were posthumously awarded the title of The Righteous Among The Nations for their deeds.

The author has been living in the Unites States for many years and her everyday language is English. Nevertheless she wrote her book in Polish and published it in Poland. By doing so she wanted the Polish people to understand the memories of her past.

In the series "Polish Jews" we readily emphasize the word Polish, believing that at least in memories Poland is multinational.

Zbigniew Gluza
(The Publisher of Osrodek Karta.)

1.The family Kon: mother Leonia, born Szpitbaum, father Daniel Hipolit, Halina (the author) and her brother Jerzy, summer 1927.

2.Halina with her brother Jerzy in Czarniecka Gora, summer 1937.

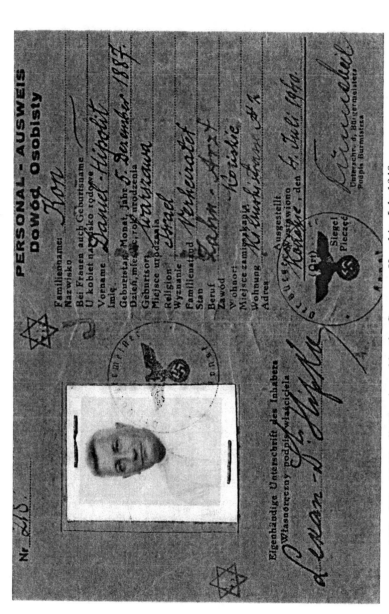

3. ID of Daniel Hipolit Kon issued by the Germans, Konskie, July 1940.

4. Halina with her half sister Helenka in Konskie. 1941.

5. Halina in Konskie, 1941.

6. Karolina Slowik, Starachowice, August 1944.

7.Olga (Dziunia) Slowik, Starachowice , August 1944.

8. The titles of "The Righteous Among The Nations" issued by Yad Vashem to Karolina Slowik and her daughters Olga (Dziunia) and Maria Kamer for saving Halina's life during the WWII.

ESCAPE TO THE ARYAN SIDE

I was born and grew up in Konskie, a small town in central Poland. There I was caught by the Second World War and in March, 1942, imprisoned in the Ghetto. Eighteen months later, the threat of the liquidation of the Konskie Ghetto became heavy in the air.

It seemed to me that during the time I had been in the Ghetto, I became resistant to hunger, cold, filth and darkness. Somehow I had escaped the devastating Ghetto diseases and death. I hadn't fallen ill with typhoid, spotted fever or dysentery, although many victims of these epidemics were lying in the courtyards covered by newspapers. I had escaped German bullets; I hadn't been injured by random gunfire. I had managed to stay in the Konskie Ghetto successfully avoiding the constant deportations.

All the disastrous events that fell with increasing frequency and intensity on the imprisoned Jews seemed to be less tragic than the present threat of liquidation of our Ghetto. This small section of town with its inhabitants was the only place on earth where I belonged. My family, my friends all lived in this crowd of people systematically being destroyed by the Germans. There I knew everybody and everybody knew me. There I tried to survive each passing day as did the Jews around me.

A growing fear of the approaching deportation overwhelmed all of the people concentrated in this small part of the city assigned to the Jews by the Germans. The existing life, in complete isolation from the Poles, saturated with the daily fear of impending new disaster, suddenly seemed much more bearable than the threat of deportation to unknown camps. The thought of being forced to leave the Ghetto, of being separated from the people I had always been with, to be transported to the hard conditions of the labor camp had been filling me with indescribable horror. I had heard, over and over again, about the liquidation of neighboring ghettos in the

1

surrounding cities and towns followed by the deportations of the Jews who had lived there. The ghettos in Opoczno and Skarzysko (1) no longer existed. A few people, who had managed to escape from these places during their destruction, found a temporary refuge in our ghetto. They talked about the incredible murders committed by the Germans and their collaborators. They portrayed the streets covered with blood and dead bodies lying all over. They described the families whose members were separated from each other; the young from the old and the children from their mothers. They talked about distant labor camps in unknown locations. They all agreed that only the young and healthy people would have a chance to survive the hard work and the cold of the approaching winter. However, the fate of the remaining, particularly children and older people, was hopeless.

One night Hanka, a girl from Szydlowiec (1), I had befriended during the summer of 1939 in the town of Czarniecka Gora, knocked at our door. Hanka was a beautiful blue-eyed blonde and she looked like a typical Aryan girl. She was lucky enough to have obtained a Polish birth certificate and to have escaped from the Ghetto in Szydlowiec, a day before its liquidation. Having no place to go and knowing no one who could help, she had hidden in the local forest for a few days. There, the Polish peasants had found her robbed and raped her. Badly bruised, dirty, hungry, looking like a hunted animal, she had run for her life. Exhausted and terrified, she blamed herself for everything that had recently happened to her. She thought that her good looks, which had attracted men, were to be blamed for her misfortune. She wanted us to help make her face ugly.

We spent the night together. We washed her stained underwear and repaired her torn clothes. We cried for what we had already lost as well as for what our unknown future could yet bring us. The next morning Hanka left Konskie in spite of her tragic experience on the Aryan side. She was

2

afraid to stay even one more day and perhaps be caught up in the liquidation of our Ghetto.

The past years of war had taught me how systematically cruel the Germans were. News accounts about their actions in the adjoining Jewish communities made it obvious that soon the liquidation of our Ghetto must follow. However, against all logic and experience, I kept deluding myself, as did many other people, into believing that for some reason the Konskie Ghetto would be spared from destruction.

Sometimes, I even convinced myself that German difficulties on the Eastern Front would force them to postpone the liquidation of our Ghetto until the coming spring. This season had a magical meaning. I, as well as others, believed that during the time when nature was reborn after the winter cold, justice must emerge victorious over crime. That spring of 1943, the hoped-for season of German defeat, would arrive in only a few months.

During the last week of October, 1942, every day we heard the rumor that Latvians had been seen in Konskie. Everybody knew how significant and cruel a role they had played in the liquidation of the neighboring ghettos and how many atrocities they had committed against the Jews. The presence of Latvians in our town could only mean the time of the action was very close. Luckily, so far all of the rumors about their arrival had been found to be false.

On October 31, 1942, the paralyzing news about the presence of Latvians in Konskie was spread to such an extent that no one in the Ghetto was talking about anything else. My family gathered in our one room apartment located at Number Four Pilsudski Street. We nervously waited for either confirmation, or hopefully, denial of this dreadful information.

My friend Jakub Lejbusiewicz, called Jack for short, a member of the Ghetto police, went to check on this news in the Jewish police station. He was a German Jew. His whole family had been expelled from Essen in Germany before the war. They had been forced, as had many other German Jews of Polish origin, to live on the strip of land between Poland and Germany. This stateless zone was a no-man's land. Neither Poland nor Germany allowed these people to enter their territory. Finally, after several months of living in this manner, Jack's family obtained permission to come to Poland and settle in Konskie.

On this day, Jack repeatedly reassured us that the news about the appearance of Latvian soldiers in Konskie was groundless. None of the Jewish police, not even his brother the Chief Commander of the Ghetto Police, had received any instructions about a special action. It was already dark outside when Jack returned directly from the police station. Unlike the other times, he immediately announced, "A few minutes ago we received the official news that the Latvians have arrived in the city. Halina, you must run away right now."

Everyone in the room, shocked and terrified by this announcement, surrounded Jack. Only Helenka (2), my five-year-old half sister, sensing the danger, came closer to me as if seeking my protection. Her childhood had been spent in the overcrowded courtyards of the Ghetto. The atmosphere of constant fear and nervousness had marked her character. She was a very quiet, timid child always giving way to everyone and hiding away in dark corners. Usually, adults did not have the time or patience to pay attention to her and she had learned to take care of herself. I loved Helenka very much. Whenever possible, I tried to bring her joy and thus brighten her too serious face with a smile. She had responded to my attention with affection. She became very attached to me.

Helenka's mother, forty-year-old Sara (3), was in the circle around Jack. One year after my mother died (4), my father (5) married my mother's niece. Therefore, Sara was not only my stepmother, but also my first cousin. Our relationship was not good for many years and improved only after the war had started. During the difficult times of my father's long illness, I

4

learned to appreciate Sara's constant efforts to save her husband and ease his suffering. She often went outside the Ghetto, risking her life in order to smuggle in a Polish doctor, to acquire badly needed medications or trade items for food. After my father's death, the everyday difficulties and the common danger united the two of us even more. Together we tried to get food for our family and protect Helenka from hunger and peril.

Miriam Szpitbaum (6), Sara's sixty-year-old mother, was one of our household. At the beginning of the war, she and her husband Moses, my mother's brother, left the City of Radom, where they had lived for half a century and moved in with us. Miriam became a widow in the Konskie Ghetto. Moses died of a sudden heart attack during my father's funeral.

Izio also belonged to our five-member household. He was a thirty-year-old, very good looking, dentist from Warsaw. My father had employed Izio as an assistant in his dental office when he became ill. After my father's death, Izio was no longer able to leave the Ghetto in Konskie and return to his native Warsaw. Thus he, too, had to stay with us.

For some time, we all had tried, as had many of the other Jews in the Ghetto, to be prepared for the worst. We slept completely dressed and wore several layers of clothing during the day. Rucksacks, packed with woolen underwear, spare clothes, best shoes and dry food for a long journey were always kept near our beds.

Many Jews in the Ghetto had constructed special hiding places to protect the most threatened people in the event of a Ghetto liquidation. It usually consisted of a closed space with a masked entrance to a storage cabinet, a corner in a basement, an end of a corridor or a part of a room separated from the rest by big furniture. A hiding place in our house was constructed in the attic. A new wall had been added across it and the space thus created was not visible from the outside. Ventilation was provided through the roof. A small opening was left in the wall for people to crawl in and close it from the inside.

Some people in the Ghetto dug underground tunnels which lead from one house to another. There was a corridor a few hundred yards long, wide enough for a grown man to crawl along, which lead from our courtyard to the field outside the Ghetto.

Young people planned to escape into the surrounding Konskie forest. Izio organized a group of boys and girls who were ready to joint the partisans. For many weeks he tried to make a connection with the members of the Polish Socialist Party and through them with the forest group. However, his efforts did not bring about positive results.

The Aryan-looking women bleached their dark hair blond. It was commonly known that they planned to escape from the Ghetto to the Polish world generally called by Jews the "Aryan-side". I was one of these. According to the "experts", my face was not typically Jewish. Still, one could find some Semitic features in me. My eyelids were too heavy, my lips too full and most evident of all, my hair was too dark. Unfortunately, I was unable to change my eyes or lips, but I could lighten my hair. I bleached my braids with peroxide until they became light blond with reddish accents.

I considered my fluent knowledge of the Polish language a big asset toward making me seem Polish. I had been hoping that my rich vocabulary, with no tinge of a Jewish accent, would help me survive.

During the fall of 1942, I came to the conclusion that I could not leave my life to chance and wait passively for the destiny planned by the Germans. The widely described horrors of the German action, images of drunken Germans, Latvians, and Lithuanians with their savage dogs, filled me with an indescribable fear. In light of that, the escape seemed to be easier to survive. The prospect of facing the approaching winter in an unknown labor camp without proper protection from the frigid weather intensified my anxiety. I had never been resistant to the effects of low temperature and had already been chilled to the marrow in the Ghetto during wintertime.

A friend of mine returned from a labor camp after being there for several months. This young man now looked like a human skeleton. His personality also had changed completely. He appeared mentally ill. He was afraid of everybody and everything. Although he didn't want to talk about the time he spent in the labor camp, his general state of mind and appearance projected a dreadful picture of it.

Helenka's safety concerned me very much. I was afraid that this child, lacking the proper nourishment for the last several years, would not withstand the hard conditions in the camp. I was sure the life of the children was very difficult there.

I tried to convince Sara to join me in escaping from the Ghetto to the Aryan side. She had a typical Polish face. Many times in the recent past she had been stopped by the police in the Ghetto and had to prove that she was indeed a Jewess and not a Polish smuggler. In the beginning, Sara did not like my plan and categorically refused to take part in it. She did not want to leave her mother alone. She did not foresee a life-threatening danger for either herself or her family in the Ghetto. She was afraid that the risk involved in an escape to the Polish world was greater than remaining where she was. Eventually, the constant pressure of my arguments and my threat of escaping without her, but with Helenka, finally paid off. Sara agreed to join my plan.

Our plan was to stay in the Ghetto as long as possible and run away only at the last moment before its liquidation. My father's friend gave us three authentic birth certificates for Sara, Helenka and me taken from the archives of Konskie.
Another friend, Doctor Narbutowicz, introduced his co-worker, Jan (7), to us. Jan would allow us to come to his house immediately after leaving the Ghetto. He also agreed to transport us later to Czarniecka Gora, a town twelve

kilometers from Konskie. Once there, we planned to spend some time in Stan's (7) house. Stan, an organ player in the local church, was Jan's closest friend. Finally, we would go to the city of Radom where Stan's friends would help us settle. Both, Jan and Stan, were paid handsomely in advance for their participation in our rescue.

In this way, we prearranged the first, and as I had imagined, the most difficult step immediately following our hoped-for escape from the Ghetto. We decided that we would run away together, but for safety reasons we would separate from each other later on. I was convinced that I would be able to find a job and a place for myself among thirty million Polish people.

I learned several Catholic prayers. I had a prayer book, a rosary and a cross on a silver chain. The suitcases, packed with appropriate clothes, had been moved to Jan's several weeks earlier. There were, among other things, the winter coats. At the beginning of the war, the Germans had confiscated everything made of animal fur. A death penalty had been imposed for the possession of any kind of fur. This German law did not apply to the Poles. Therefore, in order to look like a typical Aryan, it was very important that we acquire fur collars for our winter coats.

Since my face could still betray my secret, even though my hair was light, I planned to dress like a person in profound mourning. A long, black veil attached to my beret would cover half my face. Black stockings, black dress and a black band on my left arm would complete my mourning outfit. I hoped that dressed this way, I would create general sympathy for a young girl stricken by tragedy.

Listening to Jack's news about the arrival of the Latvians, I realized that we were on the eve of the final liquidation of the Konskie Ghetto. Though the threat of this event had been with me for at least a month, the ultimate happening struck me with an uncontrollable terror. Now was the moment of decision.

I had been hearing Jack's words, "Halina, you must run

away". I could fully comprehend the seriousness of his statement as I stared into his deadly pale face. I started to feel the heavy burden of this situation falling upon my shoulders. I would have to abandon relatives and friends, indeed, all of the people with whom I had shared all of my life.

I felt as if I would be betraying those near and dear to me by leaving them behind in the condemned Ghetto while I attempted to escape. I would have to abandon all of the things I was used to such as my folding bed which had given me an illusion of privacy in the overcrowded room. I realized how much my everyday world, which up until now I had taken for granted, meant to me. Soon I would have to enter a completely new world; one in which nobody knew me or waited for me. I was seized with an overwhelming fear destroying my self-confidence.

I began to hesitate and doubted the worth of my plan. However, I was aware that even a short delay in leaving the Ghetto could make our escape impossible. I knew the ultimate decision must rest with me. Finally, the dread of being trapped in the Ghetto during its liquidation energized me into action.

"We are running away now," I said, not looking at Sara. I started to dress Helenka.

Sara, shocked by my words, clung to her mother in an embrace, unable to separate from her. She began to cry. She accused me of being inconsiderate of her suffering. In her desperation to stay, she seemed to change her mind excessively about the need for an escape. She called the whole plan foolhardy, saying it would lead us all to a certain disaster. She claimed that instead of risking our lives by trying to leave the Ghetto, we should remain there and share the fate of all the other Jews.

Unexpectedly, Jack also started to support Sara assuring us that he and his brother, the Commander of the Ghetto Police, would protect us during the liquidation. Furthermore, despite the fact that he, himself, had brought us the news about the arrival of the Latvians, he now doubted the credibility of this information. He said, "Maybe it was only a rumor caused by common panic", which were the exact words everybody wanted to hear at this moment. Finally, Jack decided to return to the police station to check once more on the situation. Leaving our kitchen, he paused in the doorway, turned to me and said, "Wait for me. Do not leave before I get back."

Time passed and Jack did not return. Waiting for him became more and more difficult. A desire to forget about the escape and stay in the Ghetto grew ever stronger in me. The determination to go against the fate arranged for me by the Germans became weaker minute by minute. It would be so comfortable not to think about the danger and just do nothing. With all my heart, I wanted to stay and not abandon the Ghetto. I was losing my resolve. I realized that I must leave the apartment at once or I would never be able to do so later. I forced myself not to wait for Jack's return. The thought that in this way I could avoid the pain of saying goodbye to him helped me to make the ultimate decision.

Sara refused to join me at this moment, but did allow Helenka to accompany me. We agreed that I would wait for her in Jan's home until the morning. If she did not appear there, I would be forced to continue to run away with the child without her.

I hugged and kissed one person after another. The realization that I was doing an irreversible act took away from me the ability to utter a word. I felt as if everything inside me was dying. Quickly, I took Helenka's hand and left the apartment.

We walked along courtyards, called alleys, in the Ghetto. Every place was dark and deserted. It looked as though nine thousand people had been swallowed up by the earth. We were moving quickly and quietly close to the buildings. Helenka kept to the pace of my walk. We didn't say a word to each other. We passed the Third of May Street along the narrow tunnel which connected the two parts of the Konskie Ghetto. Finally, we reached a wooden fence bordering the Ghetto and the Polish territory. Here, I created an opening by removing a few loosely connected boards. I discarded the armbands with the Star of David from our coats and hid them under a stone. We passed through the opening in the fence and entered the Aryan side of Krakowska Street.

I looked around and listened for a while. The street was empty. Nobody was in sight. We walked quickly. Despite the darkness of the night, I recognized Jan's place. I opened the gate and found myself in front of a small house in a garden. The ground floor window was covered by a transparent curtain. I saw the silhouettes of a few dancing couples. I heard the sound of popular music and the happy hum of a social gathering. I stood shocked by this sight. The dogs started to bark. Jan came outside and led us to the barn. We lay down on the hay in complete darkness. Annoyed by our presence, the animals made a terrible noise. The dogs barked in the courtyard. The horses neighed and the pigs squealed in the barn. Somewhere, nearly straight overhead, the chickens fluttered their wings. I felt very uneasy on the hay surrounded by all the invisible animals. I thought about all the dogs and cats which had disappeared in the Ghetto a long time ago. They all died from hunger or had been eaten by hungry people.

Helenka cuddled next to me. After some time, she fell asleep. I lay close to her recalling all the dear people I had left on the other side of Krakowska Street. I saw Jack standing in the frame of an open kitchen door and his terrified face illuminated by the carbide lamp. His words rang in my ears, "Wait for me. Do not leave the house until I return."

Many different questions crossed my mind leaving no time for answers. Why hadn't I waited for Jack to come back before I abandoned our Ghetto? Was the escape from the Ghetto indeed a sold plan? With whom would Sara stay, with her mother or her child? How would I survive with Helenka on the Aryan side if Sara chose to remain with her mother in the Ghetto?

I wanted to sleep and not think about what had already happened and what lay ahead of me, but sleep would not come. It was very late in the night when Sara entered the barn. She told me that soon after I left, Jack returned and confirmed the presence of Latvians in Konskie (8).

---

(1) Opoczno, Skarzysko, Szydlowiec were the small cities in the neighborhood of Konskie.

(2) Helenka, born May 24, 1937 in Radom.

(3) Sara, born November 11, 1902 in Radom.

(4) Leonia Kon, born Szpitbaum in 1885 in Warsaw, died February 24, 1935.

(5) Daniel Hipolit Kon, born December 5, 1887 in Warsaw, died June 15, 1942 in Konskie.

(6) Miriam Szpitbaum, born in 1882, was murdered by the Germans in 1942; Mojzesz Szpitbaum, born in 1880 in Warsaw.

(7) Jan and Stan are fictitious names; I don't remember the real ones.

(8) From November third through the seventh, 1942, nine thousand Jews were deported from Konskie to the death camp of Treblinka and six hundred Jews were shot in the Ghetto during its liquidation. Bulletin of ZIH (The Jewish Historic Institute) in Warsaw, #15-16/1955.

THE FIRST HOURS IN THE POLISH WORLD

It was still dark outside when Jan came to take us from the barn. A one-horse cart, almost completely filled with a long wooden coffin, stood in front of his house ready for us to ride. Jan's son, a teenager, was sitting in front of the wagon with reins in his hands. At the rear behind the coffin there was barely enough space for the three of us to sit.

The cart rode slowly in the dusk along the empty streets of Konskie, with dark buildings and closed doors. We passed Krakowska and Pocztowa Streets and an old church with round clocks on four sides of its tower. We were driving under a double row of big chestnut trees on a carpet of colorful leaves. We left behind the big mansion and the surrounding gardens of Count Tarnowski. This part of the city called "behind the palace" was the area for strolls and social meetings.

Although I was looking at very familiar places, I had an eerie feeling that I had been magically transported to an alien, unreal territory. How clean, quiet and beautiful this part of the city was. How peaceful the life of the people here seemed to be. How different this place was from the one I had come from. Two totally unlike worlds were to be found in this one small city close to each other.

Gradually, there were fewer and fewer buildings and more and more gardens and small plots. We crossed the railroad tracks and we were leaving the suburb of Konskie.

Suddenly ahead, at a distance of a few hundred yards, I saw a squad of German military policemen barring the road. Their faces were turned in our direction and I had the impression that their guns were aimed at the approaching wagon.

Paralyzing fear prevented me from making any movement. I saw as through a clouded film Sara's terrified face and Helenka asleep.

The sight of the German police did not affect our driver's

13

behavior. The boy rode straight to the German lines with unchanged speed. The cart reached the first row of the Germans. We were so close that I saw their penetrating stares and I felt their breath on my face.

The commander of the squad looked at the coffin, then at us, a family in mourning, and without a word made a hand signal. The German soldiers stepped aside forming a narrow passage for us to ride through. Now the boy rode very slowly moving along the endless number of soldiers. When we passed the Germans and were some distance ahead of them, I saw them still watching our wagon with their guns pointed at us.

After a few hours, we reached Czarniecka Gora. It was a summer resort where, for many years, we used to spend our vacation in a rented peasant house. According to our prearranged agreement, we arrived at Stan's, a church organist. It was November 1, 1942, All Saints Day, a holy day marked by social visits. To avoid being recognized, Stan cautioned us to stay in the separated, closed room while his guests were in the house. He also advised us to remain with him overnight and leave by train in the early morning. He referred us to his friends in the City of Radom, who would be willing to help us settle in that place. Our host made a very good impression on us. He appeared to be a warm and sincere person and we were full of hope for the future.

In the evening, we were invited to supper with the host's family. Everybody got a big plate of hot, red borsch. In the middle of the table was one big bowl of potatoes seasoned with lard. We ate the soup and the potatoes with the same spoon. Traces of borsch left red spots on the snow-white potatoes.

I fell asleep very quickly after this wonderful feast. Male voices, coming from the adjacent kitchen, awakened me. The door between our room and the kitchen was not completely sealed. A narrow beam of light came through the crack under the door. The conversation was loud enough so that I could hear occasional words. Suddenly, I heard somebody mention my real last name. This aroused me and I started to pay closer attention. At first, I couldn't grasp the meaning of the sentences, but after a short time the essence of the conversation behind the closed door became clear to me.

The unknown men in the adjoining kitchen discussed murder, a plan to kill the three of us. Our host was plotting to take us to the train station very early in the morning while it was still dark outside. All the other partners were to wait for us in the middle of the field under a large tree. Each of them had already been assigned to kill one of us with axes. The conspirators expected to find a lot of valuable things among our belongings and they intended to divide these among the four of them.

Listening to them, it was difficult for me to comprehend that they were talking about ending our lives and not about a plot in a murder mystery. I couldn't believe that I was trapped by such bandits. Furthermore, I knew that no law or moral code could protect me from them. If they succeeded in their crime, they would never be punished for it.

After the men finished their conference, they turned off the light and left the house.

Sara and I jumped out of bed simultaneously. She, too, had heard the deliberation in the adjacent kitchen. We decided to leave Stan's house immediately. Without a sound, we dressed ourselves and in a short time we were ready to go. We had to leave behind most of our possessions taken from Konskie. We knew our way. We walked very fast through the darkness of the night. Soon we reached the station. It was a simple booth made out of an old railroad car with one side missing. It stood in the open field near the train tracks.

It was the middle of the night. Nobody was on the platform. We were to wait many long hours for the first scheduled passenger train to arrive. We would be defenseless in this dark emptiness if our persecutors were to follow us here. There was a small house near the booth where the station master was working in one lighted room. It took him a long time to react to my persistent knocking. I begged him to let us in. I told him we had just returned from a funeral and were half frozen from the cold night air. He must have felt sorry for us. He allowed us to stay inside against the prevailing regulation.

Just before the arrival of the first train, we left the warmth of the room and went outside. By now, a number of people had gathered. Stan was also among them looking for us. He was visibly concerned by our sudden disappearance from his home. We gave him an invented explanation without revealing the real reason for our late night departure.

On the train platform, I no longer felt threatened by him. In my opinion, he might be capable of murdering some Jewish women in a dark field, but not in a lighted place full of people. I considered the presence of the crowd to be our salvation.

Looking down at the platform from the already moving train, I saw Stan gesture to some unknown men. Then the men boarded our train. According to the escape plan created with the help of Stan, we were supposed to proceed to his friends in the City of Radom. Now, having learned what kind of person Stan was, we realized his friends could be his partners in crime. We decided to change the direction of our trip and run away from the men following us. We left the train in Skarzysko, the first junction station and changed our destination to Warsaw, the capital of Poland. We thought that in the big city we would not attract special attention. We hoped that Sara's familiarity with the city, in which she had lived for several years before the war, would help us in many ways.

Sara went to purchase the tickets to Warsaw, leaving Helenka with me. I took a place in the far corner of the waiting room and covered my face with a mourning veil. After a lengthy period of waiting, Sara returned very upset. She told us to leave the waiting room immediately and meet her outside on the platform. There, I found out what had happened. A peasant woman, who for years had delivered dairy products from her farm to our family in Konskie, had recognized Sara. This encounter made the woman sincerely excited. She had grabbed Sara's hand and greeted her loudly, "Mrs. Kon, it is good to see you healthy and well." Kon was not only our true last name; it was also a typical Jewish name. This expression of spontaneous delight by the peasant woman could have had tragic consequences for us. Luckily, no one in the passing crowd paid attention to this greeting.

TRIP TO WARSAW

I entered the fast train connecting Skarzysko directly to Warsaw. Sara arrived with Helenka shortly afterward. We agreed at the beginning of the trip that we would pretend not to know each other. Thus if one of us would be recognized as Jewish, the other one would still have a chance to save herself. I was convinced that my face could arouse suspicion and that it was I who protected Sara and Helenka by such an arrangement.

The train car was made of several open compartments on one side while a long corridor on the other side served not only as access to the individual compartments but also to the adjacent train cars. Each compartment had two wooden benches with four seats. An open space above the seats allowed anyone to see throughout the whole car.

In our compartment, only one seat was taken. A middle-aged woman with a nice, intelligent face occupied the place near to the window. I took a seat opposite her. This way only the side of my face, covered by the mourning veil, would be visible to the passengers passing by. Helenka and then Sara sat next to me. We purposely chose this order of seating to hide my Semitic features as much as possible and expose only Sara's "Polish" face.

The train left the City of Skarzysko and moved through the countryside. The people in the different compartments started a loud and joyful conversation. The steady rhythm and the clatter of the fast moving train began to relax the tension I still felt after the gruesome experience of the previous night. Helenka, on the contrary, became more and more excited. She was unable to stop expressing her fascination and bewilderment. After her isolation in the Ghetto, she couldn't comprehend what was going on around her. Everything that she was seeing now was completely new. This was her first train ride. She kept asking questions such as, "Why is everything moving away? Why are the houses disappearing? Which moves faster, the train or the horse-cart? What was the strange animal with the horns?" An average girl of her age could not have been ignorant of so many things. Her questions were dangerous and could indicate that this child had not had a normal life either in the city or in the country. Sara was concerned that Helenka's behavior would arouse suspicion in the people surrounding us. She tried to divert her daughter's attention from what was happening outside the window by playing with her.

Time passed and I was slowly falling asleep. Suddenly, I heard Sara calling my name. However, before I was able to react, the woman in our compartment responded.

"Did you say something to me?", she asked Sara.

"No, I called my cousin," Sara answered.

In one unguarded moment, Sara had destroyed our delicate conspiracy. Not only had she called me by my real name, Halina, instead of Maria, the name in my present documents, but worse, she had informed a stranger about our relationship.

Halfway through our trip to Warsaw two Polish policemen, commonly called "Blue Policemen", entered the car. I had known them well. Both of them were members of the local police force in my native city of Konskie. As they started to check the passengers' documents, they immediately noticed and recognized Sara. They seized her with a viciousness similar to the attacks of wild animals on their prey. Shouting names, they pulled her off the bench and ordered her to go with them. Excited by their unexpected catch, they overlooked Helenka and me.

Their loud shouting and cursing attracted general attention. People from all over the coach gathered around them and demanded to know what was going on. The policemen explained that they had captured a Jewish woman, the wife of a well-known Jewish dentist in Konskie. Pushing her and shouting anti-Semitic epithets, the policemen took Sara away.

After they left, passengers in the compartments began talking, commenting on this and similar incidents. I heard many people express anti-Semitic remarks full of racial hatred. I listened to the angry voices about the arrogance of Jews pretending to be Poles and even riding the trains. Some passengers told about Jews who had attempted to escape the Ghetto and had been captured by local people. Others proudly admitted how they had helped to track down and catch hiding Jews.

Someone expressed an opinion that struck me as being especially cruel, full of deadly hatred of Jews, "We Poles are going to build a monument to Hitler for freeing us from Jews for all time."

During this conversation in which many took part, there was not a single voice raised in sympathy for the pretty, young woman who had been condemned to death in front of their eyes. Sara's five-year-old child remained in her seat. She did not cry. She did not follow her mother. She did not look at the policemen. She did not move closer to me. She remained motionless, her eyes cast down. She must have felt the threat of deadly danger. Either it had paralyzed her or her instinct for self-preservation had directed her behavior.

I, too, was horror struck. I felt as though my body had turned to ice. I couldn't breathe and my mind was in chaos. I was unable to look at Helenka or move closer to her. I did nothing to lessen the fear of this terrified child. Here were two sisters, one an adult and one a child, unable even to hold hands. We were crippled by what had happened to Sara and by the hatred of the surrounding crowd.

After a while I saw one of the policemen, who had taken Sara, running through the crowd, obviously looking for someone. When he returned from his search, people stopped him demanding further information about the caught Jewess. The Polish policeman explained he was looking for a German to whom he could turn over the Jewish prisoner. Since he found no one on this train, he was forced to transport her all the way to Warsaw. There, he knew he would find the proper German authorities at the train station. Meanwhile, he assured the passengers the Jewess was locked in a compartment from which there was no escape.

After another half an hour, the same policeman came again to our compartment. This time he came straight to Helenka and ordered her to come with him. He informed the passengers the arrested Jewish woman had confessed that she was not alone on this train but was accompanied by her small daughter. Once again, the people started to crowd around our compartment. This time it was to look at a Jewish girl.

Helenka got up from her seat dwarfed by the surrounding crowd of grownup people. There was no sign of a tear on her pale, tiny face. She did not cast one glance in my direction. She did not make a slight movement of her hands. She did not whisper a word. She followed the Polish policeman like a mechanical doll. In a second, Helenka disappeared from my view. There was only an empty space where she had been seated a moment ago. I was petrified in my seat.

The passengers on the train returned to their places while loudly discussing the latest event. I did not hear any word of indignation at the cruelty of German laws which condemned this little girl to death. No one expressed sorrow for her short life. No one even mentioned that she was pretty and sweet, adjectives commonly used to describe a five-year-old child. For them, the Jewish children did not come under these criteria. I heard no sympathy for a young mother who must have been aware of the terrible fate awaiting her child.

Suddenly, the woman seated in our compartment looked at me very critically and lowering her voice, she stated, "You are a cousin of the arrested woman. That means that you are also a Jewess."

"Yes, that is correct," I answered looking straight in her eyes.

"Follow the policeman and tell him about me. You now have

a chance to denounce a Jewish girl. You don't even have to hurry because I cannot escape from this moving train."

I saw the effect my words had on her – something like surprise or embarrassment. She moved to the corner of the bench, closed her eyes and pretended to fall asleep. She stayed this way until the end of the trip never leaving her seat nor looking at me.

Her unexpected remarks roused me from the numbness that had possessed me after Sara and Helenka had been taken. I had only been in the Polish world for 48 hours. Yet during that time, the very people who had volunteered to help me had tried to kill me. Sara, whose Aryan face should have shielded her, had been recognized as Jewish. She and Helenka were now awaiting the death penalty for being outside the Ghetto without German permission. The Polish policemen who had fished them out of the crowd were clearly happy about their achievement. People on the train had spontaneously expressed their hatred toward all Jews. Not one witnessing soul to the tragedy of a young Jewish mother and her daughter had said a single word in their defense or expressed sympathy for the fate awaiting them.

I realized how naïve I had been when I had planned an escape from the Konskie Ghetto to the Aryan side. I did not know the Polish people. They were very different from the ones I had imagined. The Germans were not the only threat to me. The Poles, who were better able than the Germans to identify Jewish features, were equally dangerous. Unfortunately, I did not see any refuge other than the Aryan side. I tried not to think about what was going to happen to Sara and Helenka. Instead, I started to dwell upon my own present situation. Now, I was traveling by myself to Warsaw, to a big city that I knew nothing about. I had no idea where to turn after arriving there. Suddenly I became aware that Sara had forgotten to give me the train ticket in Skarzysko. Without it, I could not pass through the checkpoint at the exit.

This would make it very difficult for me to leave the train station in Warsaw.

Unexpectedly, as the train started to approach the suburbs of Warsaw, Sara returned with Helenka. Walking along the car, she stopped several times talking to the passengers. She complained loudly to them about the Blue Police, who had dared to mistake her for a Jewish woman. To me, her performance seemed very good. However, the passengers listened indifferently to her explanation. They neither commented on her words nor expressed sympathy for her "humiliating" experience. There was a strange silence in the whole car when she finally took her seat. The woman in our compartment continued to pretend to be asleep. I had the impression that no one believed Sara's version of the events.

It was evening when the train arrived at Central Station in Warsaw. We mingled quickly with the crowd of travelers. We were terrified that someone from the train, dissatisfied with the Polish Police on the train, would denounce us to the Germans. When we finally left the station and entered the streets of Warsaw, I learned how Sara had saved herself and her child. The coincidence that there had been no Germans on our non-stop train saved their lives. During the long hours when she was guarded by the policemen, she succeeded in softening their hatred of Jews by handing over to them all the jewels she possessed.

IN WARSAW

We rented a room in a hotel near the train station at Two Widok Street in Warsaw, entering our names in the official hotel register as a mother with two daughters. The woman at the reception desk appeared sympathetic to Sara's story of her husband's recent death. Sara explained she had come to Warsaw to place me, her stepdaughter from her husband's first marriage, in a convent. The woman who introduced herself as the hotel manager expressed her condolences on the death of Sara's husband as well as her appreciation for my religious calling.

Our room in the hotel was small, dark and sparsely furnished. Two narrow iron beds, a wooden closet, a square table and two chairs completely filled its space.

On the first evening, we purchased three glasses of tea in the hotel to celebrate our lucky arrival to Warsaw. This tea happened to be an extravagantly luxurious drink. It didn't bother me in the least that this tea was ersatz sweetened with saccharine. In comparison to the "teas" we could have in our Ghetto this sweet, warm, aromatic drink was unforgettably good.

We were aware the hotel was a very dangerous place for us to stay. The Germans and Blue Police often rounded up the customers of such places, checked their documents and verified identities. Now that many ghettos in Poland were being liquidated, the search for escaping Jews would be intensified all over, but especially in the hotels. However, we knew of no other place to go. This tiny room in the hotel on Widok Street now became the only place where we could rest at night.

On our very first morning in Warsaw, we bought the local Polish newspaper and searched the classified ads for all the possible jobs available which might fit us. We were especially interested in any positions for domestics which usually included room and board.

From this first day, every day we searched the city for a job. Usually, the three of us together left the safety of our room in the morning. Then Sara, with Helenka and I, went in two different directions. It seemed safer not to stay together during this search. Each of us depended on her own devices.

Sara and her five-year-old daughter wandered the Warsaw streets all day long, tired and hungry. So did I.. Guided by the addresses from the ads in the newspaper, I found myself enveloped by the people of the big, unknown city. I felt lonely in the midst of the crowd. Only at the end of the day would I return to our hotel to once again be with Sara and Helenka.

I rode the buses and the electric street cars enormous distances to far-reaching parts of the city. I climbed up hundreds of steep staircases in various buildings. I rang many front bells and knocked on numerous kitchen doors. In the beginning when interviewed, I confessed that I had little cooking experience, but at the same time I assured my would-be employers that I was able to learn very quickly. However, after several days without getting hired, I changed my tactics. I began to profess great experience in domestic work. Whatever the person needed done, I claimed to be able to do. In my own valuation, I was the best cook, the best nanny, the best housekeeper. Still, regardless of my assumed expertise and my own excellent references, no one hired me. In some places, people wanted an older or a younger person than I. One middle-aged man asked me to take off my coat and show him my figure. He explained that he needed a servant for much more than cleaning and cooking. After clarifying what he had in mind, he asked me if I would still consider working for him. One woman, who was looking for a domestic, refused to hire me because of the way I was dressed. She claimed that by wearing such a coat, I was dressed up pretending to be a lady, not a servant. "I had a bad experience with a girl similar to you," she said. "She belonged to the worst class of maids."

One young woman, a dentist, had been looking for a nanny

for her few months old baby. This lady made a very good impression on me. Her small house, situated in the suburbs of Warsaw, seemed a safe place to stay. I wanted very much to be hired by her. I tried to impress her with my special experience in caring for small children. While I kept assuring her that she would be very satisfied with my services, she stopped me in the middle of my monologue saying, "Please try to understand, I am young and have a small baby. I want all my family to survive the war. I cannot endanger them."

It was clear what she wanted to convey to me and her words upset me very much. I left her feeling completely hopeless.

As I walked the streets of Warsaw, I was always aware of the danger of being recognized as Jewish. I would walk quickly, pretending to be in a hurry, to have some urgent business elsewhere to attend to or to be preoccupied with important thoughts. But at the same time, I was conscious if anyone cast a glance at me and lingered longer than I would consider accidental. I listened to the sound of footsteps knowing exactly how long the same person was behind me. Each car that suddenly stopped close by would cause my heart to race and my throat to choke up. It would take a great effort for me to appear calm and not show my fear. I was actually aware of my sad Jewish eyes and tried to change them by smiling at the strangers on the streets as a carefree girl might do. I kept on smiling at my employers-to-be and to the inhabitants of the hotel when I returned exhausted to our room.

In a mysterious way, I knew what I was supposed to do and what I must not do. Some instinct guided me through transformation from a Jewish girl in a small town to a Polish girl in the capital city. I felt as though I had developed a new sense which helped to navigate through the streets in the Aryan world.

Sara also was having difficulty finding work. In her case, the fact that she wanted to keep her five-year-old daughter with her in the place of work was the obstacle. Nobody

27

wanted to hire a servant with a small child.

As each day passed, our situation became more and more difficult. The room in the hotel was costly and the extended stay was steadily draining the small funds we had. Just before escaping from Konskie, we acquired some money by selling the remains of our prewar possessions to Poles, who sneaked into the Ghetto to purchase items cheaply. Each of us also had two gold rubles sewn in our coat seams. My father had purchased this gold money a long time ago and kept it for a "rainy day". The gold was hidden in a recess constructed for this purpose in the linen closet. When I was a small child and no one was around, I used to take the coins from their hiding place and admire the shine of the pieces. I was fascinated not only by their beautiful color and mysterious value, but also by the secret manner in which they were hidden. When it came time to leave the Ghetto, we knew that the "rainy day" had come and we decided to divide the golden coins among the family members. This money could help us in our present financial situation. However, we knew neither its value nor to whom we could safely sell it.

Yet with the passage of time spent in Warsaw without having any way of earning a living, we became even more careful in spending the little money we had. Instead of eating soup twice a day in the nearby shop, we reduced this hot meal to only one in the evening.

Several months earlier when we were preparing our escape from the Ghetto, my father's Polish friend, Dr. Jan Wylezynski, gave us the address of his Russian acquaintances in Warsaw. According to him they were decent people with whom we could talk openly. We decided to find them and appeal for help. The Russian woman sympathetically listened to our story. It looked as if she understood the gravity of our situation. She promised to look for some kind of paid work for each of us. Her willingness to help gave us hope and improved our frame of mind.

My eighteenth birthday happened to be at the beginning of November. However, I did not feel eighteen. I did not even feel young at all. Three years of war had aged me and made me very adult. The responsibilities I felt I had, for myself, Helenka and Sara, made me extremely serious. My character had changed. I lost the sense of joy and humor which I had had before. I often felt tired. The evening of my birthday, we celebrated by enjoying the delicious tea from the kitchen in the hotel and recollecting pleasant moments of the past.

One evening, completely unexpectedly, a Gestapo and a Polish policeman, accompanied by the hotel manager entered our room. The policeman requested our documents and scrutinized the birth certificate under my assumed name of Maria Nowakowska very carefully. Suddenly he asked me when I would celebrate my name day.

"Pretty soon, it is on December 8. Do you want to wish me a happy name day?" I answered with an easy manner and a laugh.

The policeman returned our documents and all of them left the room.

It just so happened that only one day before this inspection by the Gestapo I had learned Maria's name-day from Sara. It was celebrated only by Poles and not by Jews. I, as well as all my Jewish friends, celebrated our actual birth date. Sara then told me a story about her student years. When the head mistress of her school, Maria, celebrated her name-day on December 8, there was a holiday and the school was closed.

Thanks to this casual comment, I was able to answer the policeman's question correctly and quickly. This coincidental information, coupled with my self-composure and unhesitating reply, convinced the policeman more about my being a Catholic than my documents. This time everything went well. We had received temporary permission to continue living. But how long could this last? Would I know the other minute details which differentiated the everyday life of Poles and

Jews? Wouldn't my eyes betray me? Would my voice be steady, not trembling? Would I be able to laugh at a dangerous moment?

My hair gave me great concern. By now, it had been several weeks since I had bleached it in the Ghetto and the roots had started to become black. I didn't have any way to lighten them up in my hotel room. Therefore, I decided to go to a professional hairdresser. I was fully aware that the black regrowth, contrasting with my bleached braids, could arouse suspicion. However, I did not have any choice. I had to take this risk and have my hair lightened. Otherwise, its blackness would become noticeable to everyone.

Sara and Helenka saw me off at the entrance of the beauty parlor located close to the hotel.

"I will return to the hotel in a few hours," I said. "Don't worry, I will come back," I assured them. But even more, I was trying to reassure myself.

I waited until they disappeared behind the corner and then I entered the shop. In a big room, a young male hairdresser was working on a middle-aged lady's hair. He placed me in a corner of the shop near the window. He listened to my request without asking questions or making any comments. The procedure took the whole day. The hot perhydrol that he used for bleaching painfully burned my skin. Worse than the physical pain, however, was a tormenting fear that was with me all that day. I didn't have the slightest doubt that the hairdresser recognized a Jewess in me from the moment he looked at my hair. What other girl could have had long blond braids with dark black roots. Well aware of the danger, I paid close attention to the hairdresser's every step. I listened to conversations he had and to the telephone calls he made. A few times, he left the shop. I watched him through the window going away. When I saw him returning without a policeman in tow, I heaved a sigh of relief. The hours of treatment passed very slowly. After the job was completed, my hair looked very nice. The color of my long, light braids seemed natural. The hairdresser accepted the agreed upon price and said goodbye without any words. I returned to the hotel completely exhausted. However, I felt glad that I had once again safely managed to get through a dangerous day.

Soon after, the Russian lady notified us that she had found a job for me. A convent located in the suburb of Warsaw agreed to employ me. It provided room and board. In a short time, the present employee had to leave and I was accepted to replace her. Suddenly, fate was smiling on me. I couldn't have dreamed of a better place. I believed that this job would mean being among honest people and having a safe roof over my head. I was convinced that it was the right place where I would be able to survive the war. In some miraculous way, Sara's fabricated story about my entering a convent in Warsaw as the reason for our arrival in this city was almost becoming true. This seemed a good omen.

Unfortunately, Sara was not as lucky as I. The Russian woman had not been able to find work for her. Sara continued to look for a job. She would meet the people who advertised for a domestic, but she had no success. Helenka, not eating properly and walking long miles every day, became more and more skinny. Her small, pale face lost its liveliness.

We came to the sad conclusion that Sara had no chance of being employed in a big city such as Warsaw. We hoped that she would have a better chance in a small town where there could be fewer people available for hire.

A few months earlier, a Polish woman we had accidentally met in the Konskie Ghetto told us about her family who lived in Starachowice, a town located between Skarzysko and Ostrowiec. Although she gave us their address, she strongly requested us to use it only in case of an absolute necessity. Sara decided to go with Helenka to that town. One day I said goodbye to them in our hotel room. I didn't dare to see them off at the train station because of the intensive police activity there.

Now I was left all by myself in the hotel on Widok Street. I felt alone in the big city of Warsaw. All I could do was passively wait until the job began at the convent.

I felt very forsaken after the departure of Sara and Helenka. For the first time in my eighteen years, I found myself without any close person around me. My extended stay in the hotel seemed to be more and more dangerous. The time was passing very slowly. I restlessly counted the days separating me from the date of my promised employment.

The manager of the hotel visited me often now. Probably she felt responsible for a young girl from a small town that lacked supervision and protection from the temptations of the worldly city. Now and then I saw couples laughing and kissing in the corridors of the hotel. Frequently, I heard the sounds of amusement and passion through the thin walls of my room. Once I noticed a woman leaving the adjoining room who, under her half open fur coat, was completely naked. The embarrassment on my face amused her so much that she burst out laughing.

Sometimes the manager invited me to her private apartment in the hotel. There she treated me to sweet cookies and encouraged me to use her library. I was grateful for her kindness, especially for lending me the books which helped me to pass the time. Although I felt safer in my room than outside of it, I forced myself to overcome fear and leave the hotel from time to time. I had to pretend that I lived the normal life of a young girl. Usually, I went for a walk in the afternoon. At that time, dusk covered my face with grayness. There were a lot of people in the streets then. I walked fast, as other people did, pretending to hurry home after a whole day of work.

One day, I saw a man in front of me whose appearance struck me with force. There was something very familiar in his whole silhouette, especially in his way of walking. His arms took an active role in the movement. First, he raised one arm high in the air and let it fall down. Then he lifted the other one, synchronizing the movement of arms with his fast, long steps.

Right arm upward, right leg forward and left arm upward, left leg forward. My friend, Moniek Finkelsztajn, used to walk in exactly the same characteristic way.

My heart started to beat very fast. Was it possible that our paths crossed in this place, on an unknown street of Warsaw? Was it possible that in this strange sea of human beings, I had found an old friend from Konskie? Was it possible that in a short moment I would be able to shake the hand and look in the eyes of a dear person?

My imagination already painted the picture of our upcoming encounter. Passing each other, we would suddenly stop in mid-step. Not believing our eyes, we would hold our breath. Not trusting ourselves, afraid of making a mistake we would examine and reexamine each other. Alert, and being as always on guard, cautious not to reveal our deadly secrets, we would avoid calling out our real names. But we would simultaneously and endlessly repeat the same question, "Is it possible that this could be you, is it possible that this could be you, is it..." Following the man in front of me, I couldn't stop daydreaming about walking together along the streets of Warsaw. I was longing for it to happen. I wanted to be with him even if this encounter would bring me tears of sorrow instead of laughter and joy. We were two friends with a history binding us. We were two people who knew each other's family. We were two escapees from the Konskie Ghetto. We were two very lonely souls lost in Warsaw.

Walking fast, I outdistanced him by about ten yards and then I stopped pretending to check the number on the nearest building. Then, as if I went too far, I started to go slowly back in the direction of the approaching man. My gaze was steadfastly on him. When the distance between the two of us became small and his whole figure was clearly visible, I saw the face of an unknown man.

I returned to the hotel very exhausted. During the sleepless night that followed, I recalled the whole history of my friendship with Moniek. I wanted somehow to be compensated with this recollection for the disappointment I had had a short while before. Moniek Finkelsztajn was a refugee from Lodz and came to Konskie in the beginning of 1940. Somebody introduced him to my circle of very close friends. He became the tenth member of our group, which now consisted of five girls and five boys. He was seventeen years old. With his dark blond hair, green slanting eyes, a sharp nose and the red cheeks of a peasant boy, he was a nice-looking young man. His face was so typically Polish that Jewish policemen in the Ghetto often checked his papers suspecting him of being a Polish smuggler. He was a quiet and serious boy, but when he was in good humor his spontaneous, loud laugh was infectious to all of us. We considered him to be an unusually intelligent, well-read and knowledgeable member of our group.

Moniek's parents were well off before the war, but in Konskie their sole source of income was from the sale of items saved from Lodz. At first, the Finkelsztajn family stayed in an apartment on Polna Street in Konskie far away from the center of the city. Very often our group of ten used to gather there in the evenings. We sat on the floor in a cozy and very clean kitchen. Usually, Moniek's parents and his younger sister left us alone there after a short time of small talk. There were shelves around the walls full of books with the Polish Great Encyclopedia in the central place. We read it as one reads a novel, and we discussed all the emerging issues. We were very hungry for knowledge and sometimes we spent whole nights reading and discussing different topics.

We were young then and our approach to relationships was very idealistic. We considered that the real beauty of our ten-person group lie in the fact that we didn't allow ourselves to have anything other than platonic friendships among us.

Regina Frydman and Samek Pizyc were the first couple who broke this unwritten principle They fell in love. At first, their mutual feelings created some embarrassment in the rest of us. We didn't know how to react so we pretended not to see the obvious. Later on, we accepted their love as normal and were even glad that it had occurred.

It was also readily apparent that I attracted Moniek's special attention. He was always looking for a seat near me and most of the time his eyes were following me. The fun our friends poked at Moniek's behavior made me very uneasy. However, neither Moniek nor I reacted to these repeated jokes. We pretended not to hear them and not to understand their true meaning.

One day in June of 1941, Moniek asked me to go for a walk out of the Ghetto. There was something so forceful in his dangerous request that I was unable to refuse. I agreed to this venture in spite of the fear I felt. It was a beautiful day. We walked along a narrow path between fields covered with tall, almost ready-to-be-cut rye. No one was in the range of our vision. We passed the border of the Ghetto, the Jewish cemetery wall, and we went farther in the direction of a distant forest. We stopped on a small stretch of green meadow, hot from the bright sun. The world surrounding us was full of the aroma of blooming flowers. The beauty of it made me recall a poetic description of nature I once read. "The earth was covered with a green carpet, decorated with the mosaics of colorful flowers; all of nature was saturated with golden rays of the sun; the transparent air was full of singing larks..."

We took our places on the grass, not very close to each other, somehow embarrassed by the intimacy of the situation. We were alone, far away from the Ghetto. We kept quiet. When the silence prevailed for a long time, I felt uneasy. I looked at Moniek and met his eyes.

"Halina," he said, "let's suppose that I love you."

"Let's suppose you do," I answered.

"No, we don't have to suppose. I really love you," he said slowly.

For the first time in my sixteen years, a boy offered me his love. He didn't tell me about his feelings on the overcrowded streets or in the dirty doorways or on the stairs, where our social lives customarily took place. For this declaration of love, he chose a place far outside the Ghetto with the beauty of nature as the background. I was taken aback by his admission. I felt proud that he offered me a gift of love, but at the same time I didn't know what to do with it. It crossed my mind that as a result of his confession, we were engaged and I should kiss him now. But I didn't do it. I remained motionless and silent sitting on the grass. I didn't know what to say. I asked myself if it was possible that I also loved him, but I was not aware of this feeling. I didn't know the answer.

We returned home along the same path between rye full of cornflowers and cockles. We were silent. We walked holding hands. I heard the sound of a train in the distance. I thought about people traveling to far away places. I was envious of them.

Moniek's confession on the meadow and our hand holding on the way back were the only intimacies we shared. Never again did we return to the topic of love and we both behaved as if our trip outside the Ghetto did not exist. Everyday life in the Ghetto became more and more difficult and I was able to see Moniek less and less often. Jack became my closest friend, very helpful and caring, during my father's long sickness. However, I was always following Moniek's life. I knew that his whole family managed to remain in the Ghetto. I heard that their financial resources were exhausted in the middle of 1942, putting them into an overwhelming poverty.

Late one evening in October of 1942, when I had been waiting for Jack to arrive, I saw Moniek coming toward me out of the darkness. I couldn't see his face from the distance, but I recognized his characteristic way of walking. He came to say goodbye on the eve of his escape to the Aryan side. I was shocked to learn that he was about to leave his parents and younger sister behind. Annoyed by my reaction, he told me that in the present situation he had to think about himself first. Though I did not condemn him for what he was about to do, it upset me greatly. I asked myself what my brother would have done under similar circumstances. Would I have been able to run away from the Ghetto and leave my father there? Analyzing these situations, I somehow felt grateful for my fate, which freed me from the necessity of dealing with such problems.

I told Moniek about my plan and the preparations I was undertaking for my escape into the Polish world. We shook hands and joked about a future meeting "on the other side". The memory of our goodbye stayed with me. The knowledge that he also was in some place on the Aryan side sometimes soothed my loneliness. Lying in this strange hotel room, I felt painfully disappointed that the man in the street had not been Moniek (1).

---

(1) A few months after I was liberated in 1945, I started to look for Moniek Finkelsztajn. I posted announcements in the newspaper in Lodz and in Jewish committees in the big cities of Poland. One day in response to my search, an old, sick man came to me. It was Moniek's father, who, after years spent in different concentration camps in Germany, returned to Poland. He also searched for his son, but Moniek disappeared forever without a trace.

Finally, my last evening in the hotel arrived. Tomorrow would be my first day of work.

Until now, I hadn't had any direct contact with my employers to be. All I knew about the future job was that the nuns of an unspecified convent at an unknown location agreed to hire me as a domestic help. My Russian friend was in touch with the Sisters, but she refused to introduce me to them before the starting date of my employment. I thought such an extreme precaution shouldn't be applied in this case. However, I had to submit to the secrecy and be grateful for what had been done for me. The most important fact was that tomorrow morning, accompanied by my Russian friend, I would go to work. Then I would start a new chapter of my life.

During the last evening in my room on Widok Street, the hotel manager brought me cookies with hot tea and she refused to take any payment for this luxurious treat. She invited me to visit her whenever I would be able to do so and she gave me a novel from her library as a gift. We said goodbye very affectionately. It was obvious to me that this woman had grown to like me and she demonstrated her feelings in a very pleasant way.

I went to bed early, but I couldn't fall asleep. I thought about Sara and Helenka, who had left Warsaw some time ago. I hadn't had any news from them and I did not even expect to get any. We had decided not to correspond with each other until we would acquire stable and safe addresses. Our Russian friend was going to be the future liaison-person. My thoughts also went to Jack and all the other dear friends I had left in the Konskie Ghetto a few weeks ago. I tried to imagine the places where they were and the lives they lived now.

Anxiety and worries kept me awake. I started to read the book I had received, called *"The Wreck"*, written by

Rabindranath Tagore. Gradually, I became drawn into the action and the time passed unnoticeably. When I stopped reading late in the night, silence surrounded me. I left the bed and went to the window. The courtyard of the hotel was surrounded on four sides by tall buildings and appeared like a deep cave. The quadrangle of houses obscured a view of the sky. All the window facing the courtyard were black and it looked as if there were no trace of life inside the rooms. I returned to my bed with a sad feeling.

Suddenly the stillness was broken. German shouts ruptured the silence of the night. Yelling exploded first in the courtyard and a moment later in all the corridors of the many-storied building. German commands, interwoven with Polish ones, resounded from all sides. The screaming, multiplied by echoes, created an impression of an army attacking the hotel.

My first impulse was to switch off the light, and in case the Germans entered my room, pretend to be woken up by them. But I changed my mind fast. The Germans might already have noticed the light in my room. Then, my pretense would be obvious and dangerous. I decided to stay in bed with my book open and the light on. Soon I heard rapid knocks at the door and before I was able to answer, a man in civilian clothes entered my room.

"Prepare your documents and get dressed," he ordered me in Polish and left immediately.

My mind started to work very fast. I knew that first of all, I must remain calm and behave as if, after the inspection of my papers was over, I would continue my interrupted sleep. I decided not to get dressed, although at the same time I was afraid of not following the order. So as a sort of compromise, I put my documents on the table and threw on my winter coat with a black mourning band on the left sleeve. In my long nightgown covered only partially by the coat, barefoot, disheveled, I stood near the table. I had an overwhelming feeling of my whole body becoming frozen, but maybe because of it I remained calm. I waited.

Two men entered the room, one in a uniform and the second in civilian clothes. The uniformed German took a seat behind the table and the civilian stood near him. A death's head on the German's cap, insignia of the Gestapo, was at the level of my eyes. They started to check my two documents. I had the authentic birth certificate of Maria Nowakowska issued by the Roman Catholic parish of Ilza. I had obtained it from the municipal archives in Konskie where it had been stored for a long time. I didn't know if the real Maria Nowakowska was dead and I was her incarnation or if I was a duplicate of a living person. The second document I had was a record of Nowakowska's departure from the City of Ilza, indispensable for my registration in a new place of residence. This last paper was false, though it was written on an authentic form. Maria Nowakowska was never registered among the inhabitants of Ilza.

The man from the Gestapo started to ask me questions in German. The civilian translated them into Polish and my answers into German. Both of the men behaved politely and were almost friendly. They started with simple questions such as name, date of birth, place of birth, place of permanent residence, and so on. Then they asked me why had I left my home. I answered I was accepted by the convent in Warsaw where I wished to spend the rest of my life. I also mentioned I had recently lost my father, hoping that the reference to my orphanhood would awaken some kind of human impulse of sympathy. During my explanation, the manager entered the room. Asked by the German about me, she stated that a few weeks ago had she met my mother and a younger sister. She also told them about my religious devotion and my plan to join the convent. I had the impression that her unexpected appearance reinforced my credibility.

The German finished asking questions and again he ordered me to get dressed.

"You will go to the Gestapo with us for verification of your testimony," explained the civilian.

After they left, I helplessly sat down on the bed. I saw the danger surrounding me and I didn't know how to avoid it. I was convinced that "verification of my testimony" in the Gestapo would prove the falseness of my identity. One telephone call to the City of Ilza would prove Maria Nowakowska was not registered under the address given. A simple question about a main street in Ilza would show that I didn't know this city at all. That was enough for the Germans to conclude I was not the person I claimed to be, but an escapee from a Jewish Ghetto. For this offense, the death sentence would await me.

Desperately, I was trying to find some salvation, but no solution to my situation seemed to exist. I was waiting for something to happen, something that would save my life. Passivity was the only defense I could see. So I didn't get dressed, as if by staying undressed I was making it difficult for the Germans to drag me with them from the hotel. I remained in my long night gown sticking out from the winter coat. I did not put on shoes and my bare feet were red from the cold. I didn't comb my hair and my long braids remained disheveled.

The time was passing. The loud German shouting continued to resonate in all parts of the hotel. Then unexpectedly, the civilian entered my room again. "You are not dressed yet," he stated, clearly annoyed by this fact.

Pushed by some sudden impulse, I moved toward him. "Sir, I was waiting for you. I know that you are a Pole and I have confidence in you. I want to tell you the whole truth, which I couldn't say before in the presence of a German. I cannot go with you to the Gestapo, but I can explain to you why. As long as I can remember, I always dreamed about spending my life in a convent. My father did not allow me to do so. Finally, my stepmother gave me permission to become a nun after his death. Luckily, I was recently admitted to a convent in Warsaw. Unfortunately, at the same time, I was notified that I was to report to Germany for work. To avoid deportation, I had to escape from my home in Ilza. Now if I go to the Gestapo, they will learn everything about me and they certainly will send me to Germany. This will ruin my calling. For me, this would be worse than death. Sir, help me, please."

I said all of it in one breath, not looking at the civilian even for a moment. I didn't want him to interrupt my talk and I was afraid of his reaction. He was either a German or a *Volksdeutscher* or a Pole working for the Gestapo. To appeal to his Polish nationality could anger him or it could flatter him. I was counting on the second possibility. In any case, my appeal to him could demonstrate a grave naiveté on my part and could indicate that what I just said was the truth. Anyway, this was the only idea which suddenly occurred to me when I saw him entering my room.

Only when I finished my speech was I brave enough to look at the civilian's face. It was calm with no visible anger. I even had the impression that I saw a kind of amusement there. He didn't say a word to me. He just turned his back and left the room. Like an automaton, I sat back on the bed devoid of any energy.

Suddenly, there was some commotion and intensive yelling in two languages close by, outside my room. I could distinguish one word, constantly repeated, in the stream of German epithets, *"Jude, Jude..."* I was almost sure that I also heard sounds of blows and a cry of pain mixed with the shouts of the commands and swearing.

All of a sudden a big group of Gestapo slammed at the door, opening it and rushing into my room. The crying and apologetic hotel manager was among them.

"I did not know that he was a Jew. He had the proper documents and he didn't look like a Jew," she kept repeating, addressing this sentence more to herself than to any particular person. The Germans completely ignored her. One of the Gestapo raked up my documents from the table into his briefcase. "You will come to the Gestapo headquarters tomorrow at nine in the morning," the civilian said to me.

All of the Germans left my room as if in a hurry. I heard their loud footsteps in the corridors and in the courtyard. Then silence fell over the hotel once again.

NIGHT ESCAPE

After the Germans left, the hotel manager came to my room to wish me good night. She advised me to go to sleep and forget about the past few hours. She assured me I would receive my documents back at the Gestapo the next day without any problems.

"It is going to be a formality. They will only check the authenticity of your papers. Some of my guests had similar problems in the past and they all recovered their documents without any complications," she tried to console me.

Lying in the bed in the dark room, I was thinking about my situation which, during the last few hours, had changed dramatically. I knew that going to the Gestapo was not an alternative for me. Even a routine check could show that my papers were false. In that case, I would not leave the Gestapo building alive.

Struggling with my helplessness, fear and tiredness, I fell asleep. I had a very strange dream in which my father ordered me to wake up and escape immediately from the hotel. His face, voice and words were clear and the whole dream was so realistic that when I opened my eyes, I instinctively looked for my father in the room.

The Germans had left the hotel at about three o'clock in the morning. Since then some time had already passed. It meant that only a few hours were left until the appointed time of nine in the morning when I was to appear in front of the Gestapo. I suspected that in the early morning hours, the manager would either supervise my departure to the Gestapo's headquarters on *Schuch*'s Avenue (1) or she would personally accompany me there. So for me, the only time to try to escape from the hotel was right now while she and her staff were probable sound asleep.

Noiselessly in the dark room, I put on as many piece of clothing as was possible to wear. Making no sound, I opened the closet door slightly and left the rest of my wardrobe hanging there. I put my folded nightgown on the pillow as I always did. I placed my other belongings in such a way that the room looked inhabited. I wanted to create the impression that I had only stepped out for a short while. I didn't take any luggage with me.

I left the room. There was silence in the corridor. I moved soundlessly in stocking feet holding my shoes in my hands. I walked slowly and very carefully, first along the corridor, then down the staircase. I stopped on the landing. On the ground floor, in front of the main entrance was a big desk and there, turned sideways to me, sat the night guard. I held my breath. His body was leaning over the desk, his breathing was regular and loud and he didn't move. The guard was asleep. I passed by him and tried to open the front door, but it was locked. I saw a bunch of keys in the slightly opened drawer and with my eyes on the guard, I gently removed them . Slowly, carefully and soundlessly, I opened the door and a moment later, I was on the street.

Around me was a dark night. There was a curfew in effect and Widok Street was empty. Moving close to the buildings, I walked very fast from one doorway to another. There, I tried to catch my breath. I listened intently to the surrounding silence. When I was convinced that nobody was around, I moved to the next dark doorway. I was especially alert at the intersections of the streets. I decided to cross over only after checking and rechecking that no living soul was around. I ran short distances on my tiptoes and then hid in black corners with my body clinging to the walls. I tried to detect the slightest sound and the smallest movement. Although I had to stop often, I advanced farther and farther from the hotel. It was still dark when I heard the ringing of an approaching street car. I understood that the curfew was over. I entered the empty wagon. Later, looking through the window of the fast-moving tram, I recognized that we had left the center of the city. It

46

made me realize that I had managed to escape from the hotel. I closed my tired eyes and tried to relax, but then the magnitude of the latest events hit me with enormous force. By some miracle, I wasn't arrested and I still was free on the streets of Warsaw, but I had lost all my life-permitting documents.

With my eyes closed, I could clearly see the German's hand pushing my documents into his briefcase. Without them, I was unable to register anywhere. I could not get a job or find any lodging. Without them, I was helpless in the event of any accidental document inspection on the street. Without them, I didn't have any chance of surviving on the Aryan side. Without them, I had to die in a very short time.

I tried to think about my next step. The Russian woman was the only friendly person I knew in Warsaw and I decided to ask her for help. I reached her place early in the morning and I waited in the vicinity until the members of her family left for work. Watching her home from a distance, I noticed Germans there. For a fraction of a second, I thought it was me they were looking for, yet I realized that it was impossible. Nobody knew abut my relationship with the Russian woman.

After the Germans left, I knocked on her door. I found her scared, upset and nervous about the Gestapo's search of her neighbor's apartment. I told her about the events of last night, though I was aware that it was not the best time to inform her about my bad luck. The loss of my documents and my missed appointment with the Gestapo magnified her nervousness. She did not want to help me. She refused to put me in touch with the nuns in the convent where I was supposed to start work. She demanded that I immediately leave her apartment and never return there again. Angrily, she pushed me out and closed the door behind me.

Outside, I felt the biting cold. I walked along the unknown streets together with the crowd hurrying to work. The clock on the nearby church tower struck nine. What do I do now? I was completely alone in a sea of people. There wasn't a single person among the million inhabitants of Warsaw to whom I could appeal for help.

There would be another curfew in about ten hours and I wouldn't be able to remain on the streets any longer. Without the documents, no hotel would accept me. I wouldn't have a place to sleep or hide. I had not appeared at the Gestapo at the appointed time and probably was already wanted by them. It was even possible that the police were looking for me in the hotel at this very moment. What should I do now? I alone had to find the way to salvation, nobody else would do this for me. I saw a hope in the immediate abandonment of Warsaw. I decided to take the first possible train to the City of Starachowice, where Sara and Helenka had gone a few weeks earlier. In the street car going to Central Station, I was seized with fear when passing by Widok Street near the hotel.

There were a lot of travelers in Central Station and being in a big crowd allowed me to regain my calm. Then I noticed an announcement train tickets would be sold only to people with the proper identification. Watching the ticket office, I saw that all of the buyers presented some papers to the cashier.

I was taken aback by this unforeseen obstacle. I did not know how I could leave Warsaw now. Then a thought of a way to bypass the German law occurred to me. I noticed that the announcement was issued just a few days ago. Perhaps, it might only be enforced at this station, but at the others the tickets would be sold as before.

The tram ride to Prague, a part of Warsaw situated on the other side of the Vistula River, took a long time. There in the East Station, the decree about presenting documents to the cashier when buying a ticket was not posted anywhere. I took a place in a long line. However, when I was very close to the ticket office, I heard the cashier asking a person ahead of me for documents. My leaving the queue after the long wait attracted the attention of people standing there. I was afraid that somebody intrigued by my strange behavior would follow me out into the street. Moving away from the train station, I constantly checked to see if I was being pursued by someone.

It became clear to me that I would be unable to buy the ticket and leave Warsaw. In my desperation, I decided once more to ask my Russian acquaintance for help. On my way back to the downtown of Warsaw, I passed near the Ghetto. I envied the Jews closed inside the walls. They were together. I wanted very much to be one of them and share with the people close to me our imminent fate. The future, which awaited them, seemed to me easier to deal with than mine because it was shared with family and neighbors. Alone, I was without any support, any encouragement, and I was losing my strength. I felt helpless. I saw that surrounded by a crowd of indifferent and hostile people, it was impossible to defend myself against constant danger.

How could I have thought only a few weeks ago that I would be able to save myself? I realized now what a megalomaniac I had been and how rashly I had acted. I, alone, an eighteen-year-old girl from a small town, tried to oppose and deceive the Germans. My own naiveté had not allowed me to recognize how powerful my oppressors were.

It grew darker and night was approaching very fast. I felt as if something was increasingly tightening around my neck with every passing minute.

In spite of my misgivings, the Russian woman opened the door for me and let me in. I noticed compassion on her face when I told her about my day spent riding from one train station to another and about my fruitless ordeals. She understood and visibly pitied my tragic situation.

There was a picture of her eighteen-year-old daughter, a beautiful smiling girl, standing on the desk. Looking at it, I got an idea. I pleaded with the Russian woman to lend me her daughter's documents for purchasing the ticket to Starachowice. But, she didn't even want to hear about her child being implicated in my plan. Then I changed the scheme. I asked her to go to the train station and use her ID at the cashier's window. I saw in this new arrangement only some inconvenience, but not a peril to her life. However, she didn't agree to this version of my plan either. She became more and more annoyed by me. Finally, she ordered me to leave her apartment.

Through the window, I saw darkness covering the city. The curfew was approaching. I hadn't succeeded in departing from Warsaw and I couldn't stay there any longer. I didn't see any possible solution to this hopeless situation. I had the feeling I had reached the end of my ability to preserve my life. Unexpectedly, the manner of my dying became very important to me. Death by the hands of the Germans appeared the most unbearable. I decided to act.

A razor was lying on the shelf in the bathroom. Some time ago, I read that an opening of veins under water is not painful. The razor was sharp and very quickly the water in the basin turned red. I did not feel any pain. The information in the book was correct. Terrified, the Russian tore the razor from me. Bandaging my arm, she cried and cursed the present world which forced children to commit suicide. She cursed me also for my selfishness and lack of consideration for her safety. I didn't cry with her. I didn't feel compassion either for her or for myself. I didn't feel anything at all.

The incident in the bathroom must have affected her strongly because she agreed to go to Central Station and find a way for me to escape from Warsaw. In the meantime, I was allowed to wait for her in the apartment. She returned with the train ticket, but not to Starachowice as I wanted, but to Koluszki. It was the only destination one could buy a ticket to without documents. She claimed that there was a connection from Koluszki to Starachowice. Koluszki was the border station between General Government (German occupied Poland) and Germany. It was known that there always was a very thorough check of the passengers.

Now I was able to leave Warsaw, but instead of going directly to the place where Sara and Helenka had gone, I must travel through one of the most notorious German checkpoints. However, I was glad that I would be on the train when the curfew arrived today. I didn't want to think about what could happen later. My train was to depart from Central Station in a short time.

I said goodbye to the Russian woman who made me swear I would forget her name, address and that she ever existed (2).

---

(1) Infamous Gestapo's headquarter in Warsaw.
(2) I fulfilled her demands. Her address, name and even her appearance disappeared from my memory. After the war, when I wandered on the streets of Warsaw, I couldn't even recall the part of the city where she had lived. The only thing, which remained vivid to me, was the picture of her beautiful, smiling daughter standing on a lacquered, brown desk.

AT CENTRAL STATION

I waited for a streetcar going to Central Station. It was an evening and rarely did a passerby appear on the empty street. Standing at the tram stop, almost without moving, I felt the sharp cold penetrating my whole body and my feet and hands becoming numb. Having waited in vain for some time, I stopped a rickshaw, a simple bicycle with a seat for a passenger. The driver of this vehicle agreed to take me to Central Station. He was a perfect driver, knowing how to maneuver between the streetcars and the pedestrian traffic. Soon we arrived at the center of the city.

The rickshaw stopped in front of the main entrance to the station and a moment later, I found myself in a big, crowded hall. The clock on the wall indicated that I still had some time before the departure of the train to Koluszki. I took a place on a bench between a group of travelers and hid my face behind an open newspaper. I felt tired, cold, and hungry. I had a nagging pain in my wounded wrist but on the crowded bench, squeezed between people, exposed to their radiating warmth, I started to relax.

"Documents, please," I suddenly heard a man's sharp voice. I peeked over the newspaper. Two men, in the dark blue uniforms of train police, called *Bahnschutz* Police, stood in front of me. I saw their eyes directed at me and our glances crossed in the air. I didn't have any doubt that it was me whom they asked for documents.

"I don't have any," I said, standing up.

"Jewess," said one of them and it sounded more like a statement than a question.

"Yes," I answered.

"You are coming with us," he ordered.

The policemen led me along the station hall, I in the middle flanked by the two of them. Tall and heavily built, they well represented German power, which grasped me now. Walking between them, I felt a kind of relief. My fate and my life ceased to be dependent on me. These two strangers had taken it into their hands. By arresting me, they freed me from the present and future difficulties of hiding on the Aryan side. I no longer had to look for a place to sleep, for a way to earn money or a way to get to distant Starachowice for help. I didn't need to defend myself against death lying in wait for me at every moment and everywhere among the Poles. I didn't have to do anything for myself anymore. The worst thing that could possibly happen to me just had happened. My nightmarish life of a Jewish girl on the Aryan side had drawn to an end. This realization gave me an unexpected inner calm.

The policemen told me that they were taking me to the place where all the seized Jews were assembled. Their duties ended there. They were responsible only for fishing out of the traveling crowd people suspected of being Jewish. The ultimate decision about the fate of the arrested depended exclusively on the Germans.

The policemen also explained to me how they had recognized I was Jewish. They told me, with obvious pride, interrupting each other and adding some details, that they were patrolling the street in front of the main entrance when they noticed my rickshaw. They saw me pay the driver and come into the station. It was already dark in the street and they couldn't see my face clearly. Nevertheless, they suspected that I was Jewish based on the way I was walking and moving. Telling me this, they praised themselves for their expertise in recognizing Jews even when their Aryan looks hindered the task. They had achieved a sort or perfection in this field, thanks to ample practice at the train station, where plenty of Jewish escapees had recently appeared. They described some of the more complicated cases they had personally taken part in without any embarrassment. For somebody observing us from the outside, we probably looked like a group of friends where the men were entertaining the young girl with amusing stories.

I was aware that I was in the final stage of my life and I wanted to share this with somebody. I asked the policemen to allow me to write a goodbye note to someone close to me. They agreed to it without any hesitation. I had the impression that they wanted to show me or themselves their understanding and compassion. They helped me buy a postcard, find a pen and watched me addressing the card to my friend Jakub Lejbusiewicz in the Konskie Ghetto. I wrote a few words of farewell and signed the card with my real name, Halina. Together we went to the mailbox and I put the letter inside.

I was conscious of the paradox of what I had done. I was sending news to the Ghetto which probably didn't exist anymore. I was informing a friend, for whom I had stopped existing some time ago, about the end of my life. I wrote to a person whose fate was completely unknown to me. However, the fact that I was able to send this goodbye note gave me the feeling of fulfilling my last duty.

The policemen locked me in a big, almost empty, very poorly lit room somewhere behind the station hall. I was left alone. Sitting on the chair, I reflected about how much time I had until the Germans would take me from here. This thought didn't create any particular sensation. I was in a state of emotional numbness as if I were drained of my life already. I waited with barely any emotion for death to come for me.

I sank into a strange state. I clearly saw my friends from Konskie. They filled the whole space around me. I heard their voices and saw their faces. Gutka and Adela were talking about stories from their past. Szymek and Samek discussed a book, walking this way and that, around the room. Jack, in the cap of a Jewish policeman, stood at the door as if guarding our safety. I found myself again among close and dear people and I took comfort from that. The sudden sound of a key turning in the lock stopped my hallucination and all the shapes and sounds disappeared. I was again alone in a strange, empty room. I stood up when the policeman came in and obediently waited for his orders.

"Do you have money?" he asked.

"Yes," I answered and gave him my purse, but I saw the amusement on his face and understood that he wasn't asking about such a small amount of money. Then I showed him the shoulder pad in my coat, the place where the Russian gold coin was sewn in. He tried to rip away the seam. But it was probably too difficult and he told me to do it myself. Giving him the gold, I felt the cold of the metal in my hand.

"Do you have something more?" he asked again.

Without a word, I removed from the second shoulder pad another golden coin. He asked me again if I had more, but when I denied it, he seemed to see that I was telling him the truth. The loss of all the money I had did not move me to anger or pity. This robbery didn't reach my full consciousness. I was still in some sort of emotionally numb state.

The policeman said something about bribing his colleague, but I did not fully comprehend his words. I was again left alone locked in my prison. I sat on the chair and the vision of my friends left in the Ghetto immediately returned to me. This time all ten members of our group (Regina, Rachelka, Gutka, Adela, Samek P., Szymek, Samek H., Moniek, Jack) (1), were with me in the living room of my neighbor Krysia, called the "Commander's daughter". Samek played Liszt's Second Rhapsody on the piano. His long fingers moved on the keyboard with astounding speed and created magical sounds. The notes, slow and sad at first, arranged themselves into a funeral march, full of the majesty of death.

Then the tones became lighter, faster, and happier until it was like a dance in the air. Finally, the music was transformed into a hymn glorifying the beauty and power of life.

I surrendered myself completely to this beautiful music. When the last chord melted in the air and I opened my eyes, the tragic present came back to me. But I felt grateful to Samek that he enabled me to get acquainted with and

56

memorize this masterpiece. I thanked him for this musical utopia, which beautified the last moments of my life.

I again heard the door being unlocked and the policeman, who had just taken my money, entered the room. He ordered me to come and I obediently followed him. He walked so fast that I hardly could keep up with his pace. We moved first along the empty corridor and then down the narrow, dark staircase. He constantly pushed me, forcing me to run, but at the same time he strongly held my arm. Suddenly, I found myself on the crowded platform. The human mass pressed in the direction of the slowly approaching train. The crowd took hold of us and pushed us closer to the incoming engine. The policeman was still near me, not loosening his grasp even for a moment. I tried to move away from him, but I couldn't free myself from his grip. He held me tightly, hurting my arm. It occurred to me that he was going to push me under the wheels of the approaching train. Before the train even came to a full stop, the crowd stormed the doors and the windows. The turmoil and noise were enormous. The policeman started to curse and scream. His sharp voice terrified the people around us and the crowd stopped motionless. I heard him shouting, "passage for me, passage for us, passage for my fiancé." People parted and I walked, pushed along by him, through the narrow path created in the human mass. The policeman opened the door, jumped in and pulled me up inside the wagon. He told me to take a place at the window and then he let in only as many people as there were seats, stopping the rest at the door. Only women entered our compartment and they calmly took their places without looking at the policeman. A blast of the engine announced the departure of the train. The policeman bent toward me and whispered into my ear, "Don't worry, the war will end soon." He kissed my cheek and jumped from the already moving train. The silhouette of the policeman disappeared into the darkness.

(1) Regina Frydman from Konskie, Rachelka Blumencwajg from Konskie, Gutka Lubliner from Lodz, Adela Rolicka from Lodz, Samek Pizyc from Konskie, Moniek Finkelsztajn from Lodz, Szymek Laznowski from Lodz, Samek Herszkowicz from Lodz, Jakub (Jack) Lejbusiewicz from Germany were all murdered during the war. Their ages were between 17 and 20.

ON THE TRAIN TO KOLUSZKI STATION

The train slowly departed Central Station, constantly changing tracks in the labyrinth of tangled rails. We were leaving the city of Warsaw, hardly visible now through the window. I was thinking about the policeman's last words that the end of the war would come in a short time. I wanted very much to believe it, but it seemed to me very unrealistic. The pending war did not look like a threat to Germans. Their power seemed to be unshaken. They appeared to feel comfortably at home in the Polish capital conquered three years ago.

In the meantime, darkness completely covered the view. The rhythmic clatter of wheels had a soothing effect on me. I closed my eyes and tried to regain emotional balance after the shocking experience of the past hours. Although I felt enormous fatigue and nervousness, I was not in a sleeping mood. In front of my eyes I had pictures of the one policeman in the dark *Bahnschutz* Police uniform, who had stopped me in the Warsaw station. I saw a tall, heavily built man with his fair hair cut short, military style, and the fast movements of a strong young person. I remembered his cold gray eyes, the expression of superiority on his face and his condemning glances. I was recalling his haughty mannerisms which made me feel like a criminal who had dared to appear at a Polish station.

The image of the second policeman was not so vivid, though the two of them seemed to be very much alike. There were some moments when they looked like a single person. When they requested my documents, I saw two pairs of widely spread legs that appeared identical in their high black boots. I had the impression that one four-footed creature was grabbing me in its claws and taking me to my destruction.

I was aware that certain features of my face could be considered Semitic. But I was not prepared to be recognized other characteristics could distinguish me from the average Polish girl. How would a Christian jump out of a rickshaw and how would she cross a street? How would a Pole sit on a bench and read a newspaper? Was the stigma of a hunted animal not only on my face, but also with me in repose and even in my bearing?

I tried to reconstruct the course of events at Central Station. First, the policemen fished me out of the crowd and announced they were going to deliver me to the Germans. However, prior to doing this, they allowed me to write a goodbye note. Later they closed me in a prison-like room and made me wait to be executed for my crime of birth. Meanwhile, they robbed me of all my money and my gold. Finally and unexpectedly, they not only freed me, but even helped me to escape.

Who were these *Bahnschutz* policemen who made a profession of their knowledge and ability to track down Jews in the crowd of travelers? What kind of people were they if they helped the Germans in the hunt for Jewish lives? Why did they rob me of everything I had? What finally made them help me to escape? How had I survived in this jungle of events?

I recalled one policeman's remark that he was using my gold coins for bribing his partner. Could it mean that one policeman was a good-hearted person, full of compassion and the second one needed my money to feel pity. Even if this was the case, the difference in their characters didn't prevent them from hunting Jews together at Warsaw's stations.

Whatever the truth was, the final result was that the good policeman allowed me to continue living and even helped me flee. I regretted that I didn't know his name. Probably, he was a Pole because when we were alone, he used pure Polish, although, in the presence of his colleague, his talk was full of German words. I wanted to believe that his goodbye sentence, "Don't worry, the war will end soon," expressed his humane side, which prevailed in him.

I tried to analyze my present situation. I was without any documents on a train where papers were often checked. I was going to Koluszki, a border station between the Reich and General Government, where without a doubt the most thorough inspections of passengers occurred. I did not have any suitcase or any bundle and this fact differentiated me from everyone in the compartment. In addition, I was without any money and I couldn't buy the train ticket for the trip to Starachowice or bribe the unexpected blackmailer.

I had to stop thinking about my hopeless situation because it made me feel as if something was choking me. It took all of my willpower to turn my attention to my fellow travelers. The women in our compartment were talking loudly about family difficulties, husbands and children, and about their commercial successes. It was clear to me they all were heading someplace in the country to buy food that they planned to sell in Warsaw. They talked about purchase and selling prices and about the places where one could buy cheaper and sell with greater profit. They shared information about ways to avoid the Germans and ways to bribe the Blue Policemen.

Their professional experience surprised me. I still remembered a common Polish attitude, very popular before the war, that commerce was a dishonest, dirty profession worthy only of the Jews. Although the anti-Semitic press called for a boycott of Jewish stores and for the opening of Polish ones, this propaganda seemed to have no influence on the general perception of the profession of trade in Poland.

Listening to this open and free-flowing conversation, I saw the women had a real fondness for doing business. Their acumen and shrewdness allowed them to prosper well and avoid all the German entrapments. During these last two years, I had been imprisoned in the Konskie Ghetto and isolated from life outside. I thought, as all others in my surroundings did, that with the Jews' detention, commerce would die in Poland. Now listening to the talk on the train, I realized how wrong this concept was. The women in my compartment were the best example that the Poles have successfully filled the void vacated by the Jews.

After some time, the conversation stopped and the woman started to prepare a meal. They removed the food from baskets and put it on white rags spread on their knees. I saw, through half-closed eyes, loaves of fresh bread, pieces of dried sausages and farmer's white cheese. The woman next to me cut smoked bacon into thin slices and put it on big chunks of bread. Everybody started to eat sharing food with each other. From time to time, somebody said something funny and then all the women burst out laughing. There was an atmosphere of a social gathering in the compartment. I was the only person completely ignored by them, as if the place I was sitting on was empty. Probably, their dislike of the policeman, who brought me here, was transferred to me. I felt the sad irony of the situation.

I was so close to the eating women, but I was separated from them by a wall of hostility. No one invited me to the feast, nobody offered me a treat, nobody even paid attention to my isolation. I was very hungry and I felt the hunger had taken control of me. The long-forgotten smell of smoked meat intoxicated me to such an extent that I became dizzy. A sharp, knife-like pain pierced my stomach. I felt nauseated. I was afraid that at any moment I would vomit in the compartment. My long-suppressed hunger, irritated by the sight and smell of these delicacies, was painfully awakened in me. I tried to recall when I had last had some food in my mouth. It was long before the Gestapo's search in the hotel, more than twenty-four hours ago. My increasing suffering made me want to steal a piece of bread, but my hands remained motionless. In my mind, I was begging the women for a small piece of food, but the words wouldn't come out of my mouth. I was sitting with closed eyes devastated by pain. I couldn't steal or beg. I was angry with myself that the principles instilled in me at home had made me helpless in my present situation.

The women finished their supper and fell asleep. Silence filled the compartment. I turned my head to the window and looked out into the darkness of the night. I tried to concentrate on something pleasant to stop thinking about the painful hunger.

After some time, the train slowed down and I had the impression that we were coming to a stop in the open countryside. The women woke up and began to pack up their bundles and baskets. I realized we were reaching our final destination. Still there was not a trace of light outside. The train was moving very slowly now. I put on my coat ready to follow the others. Suddenly I saw a long, one-story building and I read the inscription, "Koluszki". All the women in the compartment made the sign of the cross and lined up in front of the door. Following their example, I also made a sign of the cross for the first time in my life. Slowly my fingers touched my forehead, middle, left and right side of my chest. Doing this I wasn't sure if I was supposed to start from the left or from the right side. I was terrified by the thought that I had not done it properly. I looked at the women, but they didn't pay any attention to me. I lined up behind the others. The pain in my stomach and the nausea vanished.

The train stopped at the Koluszki Station.

CHECK POINT AT THE BORDER

Cold air invaded the compartment through the open door and immediately penetrated my clothes. It ran down my spine and made me shiver. Following the others slowly, I found myself on the platform. On my right stood the Warsaw train steaming with heat; on my left a cordon of police troops. *Bahnschutz* policemen, one yard apart from each other, formed a human fence restricting the passages to the platforms. A squad of a dozen of so SS-men moved along our train in the direction opposite to the one of the travelers. The Germans stopped at the open doors and inspected each vacated compartment. The railway men who followed them locked the already inspected wagons.

The crowd of passengers from Warsaw walked in the tunnel between the train and the row of police to a house located in the middle of the rails. I moved together with the wave of people and after a few minutes, I entered a big, well-lit waiting room. The warm air of the enclosed space felt comforting and relaxed me to a certain extent.

Looking at the number of people already gathered in the hall, I had the impression that the room was completely filled. But new passengers were constantly arriving and there was still some space for them. I was surprised that so many people could be transported in a single train.

The travelers, gathered mostly in groups, were behaving naturally and seemed at ease. One could hear loud greetings, occasional bursts of laughter and brisk conversations. I was standing alone and this worried me. My isolation from other people made me more visible. I looked around seeking a likely person with whom to converse. A woman near me was confessing to her friend she had numerous pieces of luggage. She was afraid that the Germans would confiscate part or even all of what she had. She was a nice-looking woman with a few suitcases at her side. I thought about approaching her and offering my help. I could take one valise and claim it as mine during the inspection. It would be better for my safety to have some luggage and the woman would have one less piece of baggage to declare. But I dismissed this idea very quickly. The possession of luggage would not by itself solve my problem. I knew that the Germans would demand documents from me and I didn't have any. I was aware of my minute chance of leaving this room as a free person and continuing the trip to Starachowice. The woman's valise would be detained along with me.

In the meantime, people stopped coming in and along with the last passengers, the SS-men and the train policemen entered the hall. The Germans closed the door and put a long table and chairs in front of it. A few SS-men took their places behind the table and the rest stood around them. The policemen guarded the exit door. Absolute silence reigned in the waiting room.

The Germans announced they were going to start an inspection and they explained how it would be conducted. They ordered us to form two lines: The right one for women and the left one for men. Every person from both lines had to approach the table, present their personal ID and their baggage. All the items had to be prepared for the inspection. Only these travelers who successfully passed the surveillance were allowed to leave the room and continue their trip.

Two parallel queues were formed about two yards apart from each other. I took a place at the end of a long, curving line. From where I was standing, I had an open view of the table and I could see what was going on there. The inspection had already started. Two people, one man and one woman, approached the table simultaneously. They put their papers and their baggage on the table. SS-men checked their documents and looked inside their luggage. In some cases, they confiscated found items. Often the Germans interrupted the search and consulted each other. Those travelers who

66

passed the inspection left the room through a narrow door behind the table. The inspection went on without any disturbance. Some people were approaching the table; some were leaving the room. The lines were slowly moving on.

Being almost at the end of the women's line, I tried to prepare myself for the expected confrontation with the Germans. I knew I had to invent some story. I did not intend to come to the table and announce that I was Jewish. But what could I tell them? How could I explain the lack of documents? What was my name? Where was I coming from and where was I going? How could I make them believe my lies? What could save me now?

There was only a small probability that the Gestapo here in Koluszki already knew that during a search in a Warsaw hotel, my documents under the assumed name of Maria Nowakowska had been confiscated. Although it seemed to me that this had happened a century ago, in reality only a dozen or so hours had passed since the Germans had broken into the hotel where I had stayed. It was still the same day. I decided to use all the personal data that were in my confiscated papers. I knew them by heart and I wasn't afraid to make any mistakes during the questioning. My name was Maria Nowakowska, and I was born and lived in the City of Ilza near the City of Radom.

This part of the story was easy, but how to explain the fact that I didn't have any documents with me? Should I say that I had run away from home to find work in Germany where I could earn some money and at the same time see the big world? However, I was afraid that the SS in Koluszki wouldn't even let me explain the lack of papers, and if they did, they certainly wouldn't believe my simple story. My eyes, my face would betray me and then they might recognize the Jewess in me. My chance of passing the inspection was very bleak.

The lines were slowly moving on. Standing all this time, I felt dead tired. I wanted to rest at least for a while in a more comfortable position but there was no seating in the room. To divert my own attention from overwhelming fatigue, I looked at the other line. There was a man over there who behaved strangely. He stood in the queue facing me as if his attention were completely concentrated on me and not on the inspection table. When I glanced at him, he smiled and gave me some signs with his hands. I was so surprised that I looked around to see whom he was signaling. The women near me were napping on their bundles and they didn't pay any attention to this strange man. It made me realize that it was I who was the subject of his interest and to whom he directed his secret gestures.

The lines were slowly moving on. When I looked again at the stranger, I saw that he was drunk. He shifted his weight from one foot to the other. From time to time, he was lost his balance and then pulled himself into an upright position with obvious effort. He was over thirty years old, of medium height and heavy build. He was wearing an expensive, elegant winter coat with a wide fur collar and was shod in knee-high leather boots.

The stranger's face warmed up under my glances. Clearly interested, he started making more straightforward signs, pointing first at himself and then at me. I sent him the most charming smile I could produce in response to this pantomime, pretending the situation amused me. I started to giggle. I let him know that I was interested in him by signaling back.

The man, encouraged, became bolder. He moved closer to me. He assured me in whispers that he had been attracted to me from the first moment. His voice and my laugh made us the subject of interest to the people in both lines, bored by their long wait. The public flirtation was probably a nice break in the monotonous evening. There were even some encouraging and cheering voices. The stranger's interest in me, regardless of my tragic situation, surprised me in a pleasant way. Somebody in this hostile Polish world liked me and was nice to me. I also saw a chance for myself in this encounter, though I did not know what kind of chance it might be.

The drunken man became more aggressive and louder with the passing of time and I responded more favorably to his attention. I tried to be very coquettish and play the role of a carefree girl. Then the man approached me with an open and unequivocal proposition.

"Come with me," he said.

"Where to?" I asked.

"To my home. I live not far from Koluszki."

"I wish I could," I answered, "but I don't see any possibility of it. The inspection will end some time in the morning and then I have to take my train."

"If you agree to go with me, we could leave this place right now."

"Don't joke, please. Nobody leaves this place before being inspected and we are standing at the ends of the lines."

"I can leave whenever I want and with anybody I please. All the men at the table are my buddies. I like you very much. Let's go now."

"I have a proposition to make." I started to talk quite loudly, laughing all the time. "If the Germans at the table allow you to go through, and if you prove to me that you are an important person here, then I agree to go with you."

"It is a deal," he said.

The stranger left me and went, clearly unsteady on his legs, in the direction of the table. All the people around us were excited and they commented on the situation. The general opinion was that the man, being drunk, exaggerated his importance, his abilities and connections.

Laughing all the time, I didn't lose sight of the table even for one second. The Germans stopped working when they saw the man approaching the table. He talked for some time directly to the SS-men, embellishing his speech with many hand gestures. His talk was often interrupted by the outburst of listeners' laughter. The SS-men seemed amused by what he was telling them. The stranger had not lied. He was a buddy to the Germans and they shared a common language. He certainly felt comfortable with them.

The stranger then turned his face in my direction and pointed at me. The Germans roared with laughter patting his shoulder with approval. I laughed along with them. He crossed the hall and headed back to me. His steps were still unsteady and he was lost his balance from time to time. He took my hand and without a word, we walked through the hall to the table. Everyone in both lines looked at us. I heard their comments and jokes. The Germans stopped their work and watched us coming.

I walked with the stranger across the long room, approaching the table and giggling hysterically. I thought about one thing only, what will happen if the Germans demand my documents. I felt as if I was hastening to my death. We reached the table. We passed the Germans unstopped. We went through the narrow door that had been opened for us. We left the station hall.

A blast of cold air cut short my laughter. We were on the platform and I saw the man's face in the dim light. He looked younger than I had thought before. He introduced himself and we shook hands.

"I live not far from here, but we have to go there by train, which is supposed to arrive shortly," he said. He seemed not to be as drunk as I had previously assumed.

"Sir," I brought myself to ask him, "I am very hungry. Could you buy me something to eat?"

He was clearly moved by my request. He handed me a wallet stuffed with money.

"Take it. There is an open coffee shop at the other side of the building and you can buy something to eat there. I will wait here and try to sober up in the meantime."

I refused to take the whole wallet. I removed from it only one bill and left the man on the platform. I walked slowly, trying to overcome the shakiness of my legs. I still visualized people standing in two lines and the group of SS-men blocking the exit. I saw myself walking in the middle of the waiting room approaching the Germans. I remembered their faces twisted by laughter and my hysterical giggling. I even smelled their drunken breath on my face.

I couldn't believe what had happened. The Germans had not stopped me. They had not demanded the documents from me. They had not recognized me as Jewish. I was able to leave the waiting hall with its long queues uninterrupted. I was alive.

I saw a coffee shop around the corner and I went in that direction. Unexpectedly, I found myself near an open ticket window. I inquired there about the nearest connection to Starachowice and I learned that the passenger train going to Ostrowiec through Konskie, Skarzysko and Starachowice was leaving in a few minutes from a distant platform. I was advised to hurry, otherwise I would miss this train. I bought the ticket paying with money gotten from the stranger. I didn't have time to buy food.

It was dark inside the train. The only light came from the poorly lit platform. The train was full of people. I barely found a narrow seat near the entrance facing the direction I was going. I was terrified that my new acquaintance from the waiting room would notice my long absence and would realize that I had run away. I knew now that he was able, with the help of his SS-men friends, to find me in this train. Suddenly, the engine jerked and the train started to move. In the first few minutes, I expected to hear alarm sirens for the train to be stopped, but nothing like that happened and we traveled farther and farther from Koluszki.

THE JOURNEY THROUGH KONSKIE

The train was moving at a steady speed, creating a monotonous clatter of wheels and a gentle swing of the wagons. It was completely dark outside the windows as well as inside the compartment. Only while passing through small stations could I see the passengers in my compartment. In this light, their gray faces with closed eyes looked ghostly. They all slept in strange positions. Some kept their heads resting on their bundles, some on their knees and some on the suitcases standing in front of them. Others slid their bodies away from the seats and lay partially suspended in air. A few of them had their heads on the closest neighbor's shoulder forming two-headed bodies.

My neighbor's head started gradually leaning in my direction shortly after we left Koluszki and finally landed on me. Several times I tried to remove this unexpected weight. The woman would awaken, mumble some words of excuse and put herself in an upright position. In no time at all her head would fall on me again. After this situation had been repeated a few times, I stopped fighting with the inertia of her head and allowed her to conveniently lie on my shoulder. Unexpectedly, this close contact with another person gave me a feeling of physical and emotional ties with the people traveling with me.

There was silence in the compartment, disturbed only by an occasional sudden snore, but this noise did not wake up the sleeping passengers. I tried to make myself as comfortable as possible in my narrow corner. I rested my head on the door and closed my eyes. I wanted very much to fall asleep at least for a short time. Only sleep could bring me the rest so badly needed by every cell of my tired body. I felt as if thousands of sharp needles were pinching me every few minutes. My legs were shaky and I was afraid that they would not hold me up when I stood. Hunger and violent stomach cramps attacked me frequently. However, my thoughts about my present situation were worse.

I was daydreaming about falling asleep. I wanted so much to forget about reality and the danger I was in. I couldn't imagine my worst nightmare being as frightening as my present life. I was traveling by train without any documents in the direction of Konskie, the city in which I had lived all my life and from which I had run away a few weeks ago.

I was daydreaming about falling asleep and being anesthetized from my painful tiredness. The last time I had had a short nap was after the Gestapo left the hotel. It seemed to me that was a very long time ago in a different world, where I still had a room and a bed. During that short sleep, I had a dream in which a successful plan for escaping from the hotel was created in my mind. I hoped that a dream in the present moment would also bring a miraculous rescue plan.

I was daydreaming about falling asleep, but sleep would not come. Instead, the memory of recent events in Koluszki appeared to me with great clarity. I saw the man who had saved me from the SS. I had not listened to his name when he had introduced himself since I was preoccupied by my problems. Thus he remained for me "a stranger from Koluszki."

At first I was convinced that he was one of the travelers, waiting to pass through the inspection, but even then I had noticed that his behavior differed from that of the others around him. He did not advance with the line, but rather remained in the same spot. He had turned sideways to the table and did not follow the activities there with the same attention as the others did. He did not carry any baggage. He seemed to be much more interested in flirting with me than in the situation at hand. In addition, there was an air of nonchalance and self-confidence about him.

Initially, I attributed his strange behavior to the fact that he was drunk. Now I had some reservations about this simple explanation. I suspected that perhaps he was not waiting in the line at all. Maybe he noticed me standing alone and purposely took a place near me in the men's line. Maybe he had been observing me for a long time before I noticed him standing there.

The scene, in which he left the queue and went straight to the SS officers, was very clear in my mind. I was taken aback by this act which smacked of drunken bravado to me. I had expected that the Germans would respond to him with shouts and an outburst of anger. But nothing like that happened. The SS-men received him like a friend and listened to what he had to say. No doubt he spoke German and was fluent in it.

The stranger from Koluszki told me that all the SS officers at the table were his buddies. I thought now that perhaps he worked with them, inspecting the travelers at this border station. That would explain not only his self-confidence, but also his ability to lead me through the checkpoint and out of the waiting room. The Germans must have had complete trust in him and did not see a need to examine the documents of a person accompanying him. The fact that he did not have any luggage also indicated that he traveled only to work in the morning and home in the evening. The wallet stuffed with money and the expensive winter coat indicated that he was wealthy. Obviously, a trusted employee at a checkpoint at the border station could have a very good income.

Why did he choose me out of the whole crowd of people? Before I started my "theatrical" performance of a flirtatious girl willing to have an adventure with a stranger, I didn't believe I looked that part.

Suddenly, a completely new, almost shocking interpretation of the whole episode occurred to me. Maybe he suspected me of being a Jewess and consciously tried to save me? A few hours earlier, the *Bahnschutz* policemen recognized the Jewess in me in a dark street. The stranger from Koluszki observed me under more favorable conditions in bright lights. He would have noticed my attention concentrated on the inspection, my isolation from the other travelers, my lack of luggage and my tired, serious face. He didn't have to have much psychological acumen to put it all together and come up with the answer of who I was. However, it was inconceivable to me that a person working with or for the SS would risk his life to save a Jewish girl while the SS and hundreds of other people witnessed what he was doing. It was unlikely that a friend of the SS officers could harbor such compassion for my life. The "stranger from Koluszki" remained a puzzle to me, but my image of him as my willful savior, though difficult to believe, comforted me.

My thoughts were interrupted by a grating sound. The train slowed and soon stopped at the station. For a moment, the light from the platform lit the inside of the compartment and I was able to see the passengers around me. Only one person wasn't asleep. It was a young man seated opposite me near the window. He was paying attention to what was going on in the station. I also wanted to look through the window and see the name of the station, but the position of my neighbor's head made it impossible. The train was already in motion by the time I was able to read the sign "Opoczno".

I knew this small town, about ten miles from Konskie, very well. The awareness of being so close to my hometown made me tremble with fear. Soon I was going to arrive at the place from which I had escaped a few weeks ago. How unaware I had been at that time of all the harrowing experiences awaiting me on the Aryan side. With what naiveté I had viewed my chances of saving myself by blending into the Polish population. How long was I going to successfully avoid all the traps laid to catch Jews? Wouldn't my exceptional luck desert me at the next critical moment?

Since the day of escape from the Ghetto, I had experienced so much that I felt old and tired, although only weeks ago I had turned eighteen.

My thoughts were interrupted by a noise outside and soon after two Polish policemen entered our compartment. They were holding flashlights and lit the passengers' faces one after the other.

"Inspection," they announced.

The passengers woke up and straightened themselves in their seats. The woman next to me removed her head from my shoulder. People prepared their documents, opened their baggage and got ready for the check. I again anticipated the end of my life. I saw a certain irony in this happening just outside my hometown of Konskie. I felt I could not avoid my destiny. I had to die where the people closest to me had perished. I felt my body becoming numb as if I were completely paralyzed. I couldn't breathe and my gasping for air sounded like a cough. My whole body was unable to move and a grip of fear took hold of my throat. I noticed that the man at the window was now so deeply asleep he even snored. Since I saw him watching the station in Opoczno a few minutes ago, I knew his sleep was a pretense. The company of another person, who tried as I did to avoid the inspection, did not bring me any relief.

The policemen started to check the documents of the passengers seated on the opposite bench and they slowly moved from the door to the window. The sleeping man was fourth in line to be checked, while I would be the next or the last in the compartment according to the order of checking the passengers on my bench. The policemen tried to wake up the "sleeping" man, first by talking loudly, then by pulling on his jacket. Initially, the stranger did not react. Then suddenly he jumped from his seat, pushed down the policeman leaning toward him and ran out into the corridor. Both policemen immediately followed him shouting, "Jew, Jew, catch the Jew."

Voices broke out everywhere; most of the passengers had something to say about the person who had just tried to escape. Nobody had any doubt that he really was a Jew and some even claimed to have known it from the beginning of the trip. Somebody remarked that when he entered the compartment, he pushed his way to the window in an arrogant manner typical of Jews. One woman noticed he slouched in his seat like a Jew and somebody else remarked on his cunning Jewish look. All of the passengers agreed he did not have a chance of escaping from the train. Nobody expressed any compassion for this human being and for his inevitable death. To them, he was only a Jew.

The train arrived at the lighted station. All the passengers gathered around the window overlooking the main platform. I joined them almost automatically. I saw the well-known station building in Konskie. I thought I recognized Danka Miller, the station master's daughter and my schoolmate, standing in a group of people in front of the main entrance. Instinctively, I moved back into the darkness. Then I saw a group of Blue policemen escorting the man from our compartment. They moved quickly along the platform and disappeared inside the building. The passengers left the window, apparently losing interest in the whole event. However, they were glad that all the policemen had abandoned the train and they could continue their interrupted sleep. The train started to move, leaving Konskie behind. People again made themselves comfortable in their seats. I still had trouble breathing and I coughed heavily. Gradually, all these symptoms stopped, but I started yawning nonstop. It must have looked very natural to the people around me. This was the second time in the last twenty-four hours that a captured man had saved my life. First, in the Warsaw hotel when the Gestapo apprehended a Jew, and excited by catching him, put off the further inspection of my case until the next morning. Now, on the train, the policemen in their pursuit of a man running away did not detect my lack of documents. I closed my eyes. I felt very tired. I knew I would finally sleep.

STARACHOWICE

I was awakened by some movement and loud voices near me. A train conductor had been informing passengers we were approaching Starachowice. The name of the city aroused me immediately. I straightened myself in my seat and looked around. I noticed in the weak glow of the conductor's flashlight that my neighbors had been replaced by newcomers. I realized that I had slept during the whole trip from Konskie. The sleep, in a magical way, allowed the last part of my journey to pass calmly and without fear.

I was approaching the goal of my journey, the City of Starachowice.

I was very lucky to end this journey from Warsaw to Starachowice, in a roundabout way through the border station of Koluszki and my home town of Konskie, without any personal documents.

In the moonlight, I could see the train was passing small houses, gardens and streets. All the buildings were dark and the streets empty. The countryside seemed lifeless. We stopped at the small station Starachowice – Wierzbnik, where many people left the train. The hyphenated name of the town confused me. I didn't know if this was the place I was supposed to get off. However, the conductor informed me that we were now in the suburb of the City of Starachowice and we would reach the main station in a short time.

The train stopped in front of a building similar to the train station in Konskie, with a big sign "Starachowice". A few people got off the train and immediately went in different directions. I alone entered the big waiting hall. The first thing I noticed was a round wall clock hanging straight across the entrance. It was three thirty. Only twenty-four hours had elapsed since the Gestapo left the hotel in Warsaw. Only twenty-four hours separated me from the moment when the Germans took my life-saving documents and destroyed all chances of my surviving in that city.

I noticed a man on duty behind the ticket window. I asked him where I could buy something to eat. I could no longer ignore my hunger. I learned that the station coffee shop was closed during the night and would reopen late in the morning. He also explained to me where the street I was looking for was located. According to him, Kilinskiego Street was a road a few miles long and ran from the center of the city to the distant forest. When I was about to leave the station, the cashier became concerned about my safety and cautioned me about penalties for being in the streets at night without permission. His warning did not make any impression on me and even sounded silly.

I walked along empty streets between two rows of tall buildings. All the entrances were closed and the windows dark. I moved the same way as I had the night before in Warsaw. I felt a strange numbness. I was not afraid of being caught. I did not think about the danger. I did not feel cold, tiredness or even hunger any more.

The night was bright and I found Kilinskiego Street without difficulty. It was a wide road leading to a forest visible in the distance. At first, it seemed like a typical urban street with tall houses and broad sidewalks. Then it became a sandy route with narrow paths. On one side of the road small houses replaced the tall buildings; and on the other, fields appeared covered by a thin layer of frozen snow.

I walked slowly along the trail and tried to read the numbers lit by the moon on the houses. I was looking for Number 4. Loud barking accompanied me all the way and sometimes a dog ran after me. When a few dogs joined forces and started to attack me more directly, I defended myself with stones.

The dogs' attacks did not arouse any fear in me, though not long before I had been afraid of all animals which, in my opinion, were always ready to do me harm. I used to pass at a safe distance from cows, horses, even hissing geese, but I had felt that dogs were especially hostile animals. My fear of dogs intensified during the years I was in the Ghetto, where the Germans at will set their big shepherds on Jews. Once hidden behind a window, I witnessed two amused Germans set a dog on an old Jew. By the time they left, the Jew's clothes and the pavement around him were red.

Systematically, the numbers on the houses became smaller. The one-story houses gave way to spacious villas surrounded by big gardens. Now and then, I had to walk inside the garden in order to check the house numbers.

I was getting very close to my destination. In the last twenty-four hours, I had overcome many difficulties to reach Starachowice. This place had become the symbol of my salvation. The determination to come to this city was the source of strength which allowed me to surmount all danger. It brought out courage, ingenuity, quick wittedness; characteristics I did not know I had. However, as I approached the end of my long journey, I began to doubt my reason for coming to this place and I wondered what I would find here.

I came to Starachowice because it was the only place on the Aryan side I had heard about. The address: Mrs. Slowik, Starachowice, Kilinskiego Street, Number Four was engraved in my memory. Maria Kamer (1), thirty years old, a typical Polish woman, blond with blue eyes, once gave me the address of her mother and sister, who had lived there since the beginning of the war. I met Maria the first time in the early fall of 1942 when she unexpectedly appeared in our Ghetto apartment with the intention of purchasing some items. I learned then that she had been deported by the Germans from Lodz. At that time she was trying to supplement her household by buying the belongings of Jews who were selling everything very cheaply. She liked our wardrobe with the big mirror, the last good piece of furniture remaining from our pre-war apartment. We were glad that somebody was willing to buy it because we were in great need of money and the wardrobe was empty anyway.

The Polish woman made a favorable impression. She showed a sensitivity and compassion for the hopeless situation of Jews imprisoned in the Ghetto. During one of her later visits, moved to tears by the terrible conditions of our existence, she tried to encourage us to escape to the Aryan side. In that emotional moment, she gave us the address in Starachowice. However, Maria strongly emphasized we should use it only in an extreme situation. She never again repeated this spontaneous gesture or mentioned her family.

Now I was on my way to Maria's family. Obviously, I did not know anything about these people. Perhaps, they did not have the same sensitivity as Maria. There was also a big difference between showing compassion in a closed room in the Konskie Ghetto and letting an unknown Jewess into their own home, a gesture for which they could be punished by death.

I came to Starachowice because Sara and Helenka had gone to the same address before me when they could no longer stay in Warsaw. I wanted to find them and be taken in, though I knew that I shouldn't endanger my dearest ones. I daydreamed about eating a hot meal with them, resting in their bed, breathing in the family atmosphere, though I was aware that I shouldn't expect too much from them. I wished that I could cry with them over my hopeless life and find understanding and advice, although I already suspected they would be unable to give me any.

I knew from my own experience how much danger awaited Jews during train trips. So I wasn't certain that they had reached this city. And even if they had been lucky enough to arrive, were they received with understanding at the Slowik's address, and if they were, were they still there? Maybe they had been turned out into the street a long time ago and the same reception awaited me.

I was unable to figure out how many days had passed since I said goodbye to them in the Warsaw hotel. There were minutes, hours and days in my recent life which seemed to be interminable. I knew that we were still in the year of 1942, but I had no idea if it was November or December.

The black wall of forest came closer and at the same time single-digit numbers appeared on the houses. I saw two identical two-story houses close to each other with the Number Four on one of them. I opened the gate and entered a small garden. A narrow path took me straight to the front porch. I knocked on the door at first gently, then more and more aggressively. The man who answered told me Mrs. Slowik lived on the second floor and the entrance to her apartment was in the back. A few steps led to the door. I had to knock for a long time until a woman's voice answered. She asked me many questions through the closed door. I had to tell her my name, why and from where I had arrived there. I gave her my assumed name, adding that I came from Warsaw to find Mrs. Slowik. I heard noise and loud conversation inside the house. Then the door opened. A huge woman barred my way. I felt her searching glances and I had the impression she saw everything I wanted to hide right away. I was terrified that this was the woman to whom I had come looking for help.

Then I heard a female voice coming from the second floor assuring Helena, this huge woman who was standing in my way, that I was expected upstairs. She moved aside, letting me pass. The woman on the second floor greeted me with ostentatious warmth, as though we were good friends. She then pushed me inside the apartment and immediately closed the door behind us.

Suddenly, I found myself in a bright, colorful, warm room and this unexpected change caught me so much by surprise that I could not take a single step or say a simple greeting. I stayed mute at the door as if I were rooted to the floor.

I was transported into a long forgotten world of light,

cleanliness, order and colors. I felt as if the closed door separated me from the continual pursuit by the Germans. The tight grip of my throat loosened, my breathing became normal and my heart stopped pounding. It seemed to me that finally I had gotten rid of my oppressors and found a safe place.

The room I entered was so bright that I instinctively looked for the source of the light. I was surprised to find that a single electric bulb, under a transparent glass shade, was illuminating the whole room. After the years in the Ghetto where the flame of a constantly exploding carbide lamp was the only illumination, this astounding brightness shocked me. The clean white walls decorated with paintings in gold frames contrasted with the bright red floor. The window was covered with tulle curtains and there were green potted plants on the window sill. Two wide beds, covered with snow white, ironed linens and two colorful carpets took up the middle part of the room. This sight was an enormous contrast to the dirty walls of the room in which I once lived in the Ghetto. There I often slept completely dressed in my folding bed covered with unwashed linens.

An older lady was sitting on one of the beds. Her pretty face was turned in my direction and she didn't let me out of her sight for a single moment. Her dark eyes inspected me very carefully from top to bottom. I felt badly dressed, dirty and disheveled under her watchful eyes. The lady's grey hair was rolled with small pieces of rags. It looked as if she were wearing some kind of summer hat. It surprised me that in this time of tragedy, women could care about their appearance and even curl their hair.

The younger woman broke the silence. "My name is Dziunia Slowik (2)," she said and then we shook hands. She was about thirty years old, blonde with reddish highlights. She had a fair complexion and was covered with freckles. She had blue darkly-ringed eyes, a sharp nose and narrow lips. She did not look like the older woman or like Maria Kamer from Konskie.

84

Her pursed lips, flushed cheeks and the red spots on her neck made me see that she was nervous and angry.

"And this is my mother (3)," she added.

I approached the older woman. For the first time, I realized I didn't really have a name. I was unable to introduce myself here as Nowakowska, the Polish name on my lost papers, or as Kon, my true Jewish name. I mumbled only Maria, the first name I had used in Warsaw. It was the only word I was able to utter. The lady extended her hand in a strange way, and only later did I realize that she gave it to me not to shake but to kiss. Although I had never been in such a situation before, I realized that I had already committed a faux pas.

There was a tense silence again in the room. Neither of the women talked to me or asked any questions. They only looked at me. I stood motionless, unable to utter even a few words, which could excuse my presence in their home in the middle of the night. I was still bewitched by the brightness and calm I found in this room. Strangely enough, I felt safe here and knew I wouldn't be able to leave this miraculous place.

Finally, Dziunia interrupted the long silence and asked me to come to the adjoining kitchen, which was also very clean and pleasant. A table, covered with a white tablecloth and a few chairs around it, occupied the center of the room. A warm kitchen oven stood near one wall and the iron bed near the other.

"Go to sleep, goodnight," Dziunia said and left, closing the door behind her. Lying in bed, I realized that I had not seen any sign of Sara and Helenka's presence. I was too tired to dwell on it.

---

(1) Maria Kamer, born 1909 as Slowik; died November 4, 1980 in Lodz, Poland.

(2) Olga (Dziunia) Slowik; date of birth, 1907, date of death, 2/26/46, Lodz, Poland.

(3) Karolina Slowik, born 1887; died August 14, 1957 in Lodz, Poland.

IN THE POLISH HOME

I was constantly having nightmares. In these dreams I was running away from the Germans or looking for a place to spend the approaching night. Sometimes the persecutors allowed me to slip away from their traps only to catch me later in another place. Sometimes people took me into their homes, but soon they threw me back into the street again.

I dreamed I was hidden behind a closet in the attic of a home in the Konskie Ghetto. A Polish policeman found me there and painfully holding my arm led me to the Germans. I begged him to let me go, but he ignored my pleading. Suddenly, I realized my voice was soundless.

A crowd surrounded me on a Warsaw street, taunting me and scoffing at all the Jews in hiding. They viewed me from all sides. They were angry with me for being a Jewess and attempting to look like a Polish girl.

The Gestapo found out I was staying in the hotel without documents. They ordered me to dress and follow them to their quarters in the Avenue of Schuch. I didn't want to and they dragged me barefoot in my nightgown through the snowy streets.

Germans used me as a ball in a game on a paved courtyard. I saw the death's head on their crooked caps while I flew high in the air. I heard their laughter and saw their faces when I fell down, bouncing on the hard stones.

I was in a small town. Falling snow covered the street. It was late in the evening. The curfew was approaching. I could not find anywhere to take refuge for the coming night. All the gates were closed. Nobody wanted to answer my knocking. Precious time was passing and I was still in the street. Helpless, I sat on the sidewalk covered with wet snow. I was slowly turning into ice.

As one gruesome dream ended, it was followed by another, all similar, all full or horror. The oppressors and places changed, but the feeling of fear and helplessness remained the same. My own cry woke me many times, but when I opened my eyes and saw the unfamiliar place, I did not want to open them again. Sometimes I heard a strange woman's voice saying I should wake up. I wanted to ask her to free me of my sleep and the gruesome dreams, but I couldn't emit a single sound.

Once, it seemed to me that a girl with blond hair lit a fire in the room. The image of her was very real. I felt the warmth of hissing flames all around me. I was afraid that the place I was hiding in was burning. I tried to run away and cry for help, but I was immobilized by fear. I couldn't do anything but wait for the inevitable.

Finally, the nightmares ceased. I woke up and looked around. At first I did not know where I was, but soon I recalled the arrival to Starachowice and my entry into the home of two strange women. Then I saw them both standing near me and immediately I dreaded that they would order me to leave their home.

However, I forced myself to smile and seeing a bright day, I apologized for staying in bed so late . I was embarrassed to learn that I had slept for forty-some hours. Dziunia told me she had tried unsuccessfully to wake me up because I often cried aloud and such sounds could alert the neighbors.

Later, the ladies invited me to dinner. The sound of this word and then the sight of the food aroused in me such an enormous hunger that I had to use all of my willpower not to grab the bread that was lying on the table. I was disappointed when I saw the level of served soup reaching only half of the bowl. I immediately wanted to ask for more. Although my attention was mostly concentrated on food, I noticed that my behavior at the table was being scrutinized by the older lady. Her critical glances made me wait for her invitation to start and to eat more slowly. I carefully raised each spoonful to my mouth, trying to overcome the trembling of my hands and the painful cramps of my stomach. The taste of the soup was wonderful. I couldn't recall anything so delicious in my whole life. A few spoonfuls caused a feeling of fullness, and after that, I was unable to eat more.

Both ladies were neatly dressed. Their hair was nicely arranged, faces powdered and lips colored with red lipstick. Their looks and manners made an elegant impression. Dziunia engaged in small talk at the table. I also took part in it, praising the dinner, the apartment and the kindness of both ladies. I kept smiling, trying to keep the conversation pleasant and far from more serious topics. Both women decided to call me Maryla, a nickname for Maria, in response to my request. Dziunia wanted me to call her by her first name also because "it would look more natural in the eyes of the neighbors," as she put it.

The hostesses informed me they were expecting some guests today. I was very happy to learn Mrs. Petronela and her daughter were coming for a visit. Pertronela Rudna was Sara's Polish name. The news that they had reached this place and were living safely in the city filled me with hope for my own future.

I asked the older lady for permission to cleanup after dinner. My desire to help surprised her. I did all the work well and fast. It made me feel good to see approval in her eyes and hear praise.

The reunion with my family was very emotional. Sara and Helenka had lost a lot of weight since our separation. They both had sallow faces and sunken eyes. Sara now had a lot of gray hair and deep wrinkles on her cheeks. She looked much older than a woman of forty. Helenka, excited by our unexpected meeting, didn't want to leave my lap for a single moment. Her small face trembled from swallowed tears and restrained cries. She constantly touched my face and hands, but never pronounced my first name. She knew too well that she could not call me by my real name in any situation and she probably couldn't get used to the assumed one. Sara was happy to see me, but the fact that I had appeared in Starachowice worried her. She understood that only something of a very serious nature could have made me leave Warsaw and come to Starachowice. She was surprised to see that during the last few weeks my features had become sharp, making me look older than I was.

Sara, prompted by both ladies, told us about her life in Starachowice. She rented a room in an apartment house of workmen, thanks to Stanislaw (1), Dziunia's good friend. Now she was officially registered there. She told everyone she was the wife of a Polish officer who hadn't returned from the military campaign of 1939. She let people know that because of the threat of being arrested she had to leave her home in Warsaw suddenly and without any luggage. This story was very probable and there were similar cases commonly known.

However, Sara felt a growing distrust among the neighbors. They were especially intrigued by Helenka's behavior, which was different from that of their own children. Helenka preferred to stay at home with her mother rather than play with children her age in the courtyard. She also seemed to be naughty, avoiding grownups and not answering their inquiring questions.

The owner of the apartment was excessively interested in everything regarding the new tenants, though their religious life and the regular attendance of church services were the main subject of her curiosity. She insisted on going with them to confession and communion at least every Sunday.

There was an increasing isolation around Sara. The neighbors ceased talking when she came near them, unlike the first days of her presence there. Now nobody invited her, nobody visited her. She could not find any way of earning money, though she asked everybody for work and was willing to take any job. She had the idea of teaching the neighborhood children, who were out of school, for a small fee, but she had no offers. Thanks to Stanislaw, she was able to sell one of two golden coins, but the money was spent quickly for food, rent and other important necessities. Sara thought her condition in Starachowice was difficult and also dangerous because of the increasing suspicions of the neighbors.

Both Slowik ladies saw Sara's situation in a much more favorable light. According to their interpretation, the sudden appearance of a strange woman with a child in a small town such as Starachowice evoked a natural interest in the inhabitants. They did not see any danger in it and they attributed Sara's anxiety to her hypersensitivity. The ladies were convinced that the neighbors would change their attitude as soon as they got to know Sara better and would even accept her into their circle. Dzunia assured Sara that her Aryan appearance and pure Polish made any suspicions of her being Jewish ridiculous.

Sara's story upset me very much. I did not view her situation as optimistically as my hostesses did. As I saw it, the neighbors suspected her of being a Jewess and the growing cloud of their suspicion made the whole situation very dangerous. Under these circumstances I could not count on Sara's help. The realization that I still had no place to go, no person but myself to rely on depressed me enormously.

Then Dziunia asked me to explain why I had appeared so unexpectedly in her home. I started by saying that I couldn't remain in Warsaw because I had lost all my documents there. However, as I began to explain how it had happened, an inner voice prevented me from being completely candid. I thought that as the proverbial drop of water could fill the jar to overflowing, the truth could mean one too many dangers for the Slowiks to face. So I concealed from them that the Gestapo had taken my documents and that I had not reported to Avenues of *Schuch* as ordered. Instead, I said that my documents were stolen from me on a Warsaw street. Then I

91

described honestly what had happened in the last few days. I told them about the loss of the promised job, the difficulties of leaving Warsaw and the long trip to Starachowice.

In telling them my story, I felt the unending danger I had experienced and my own hopelessness. I saw my emotions reflected on the faces of my audience. There was silence in the room when I finished, as if my ordeals made it impossible for them to speak. Dziunia broke it by telling me she would spare no pain to provide me with new documents.

Before I had time to thank Dziunia for her promise, Sara announced that curfew was due shortly and she immediately left with Helenka. Sara's sudden departure took all of us, but especially my hostesses, by surprise. Both ladies had been expecting she would take me to her place and that I would leave their home that night. They had not invited me to stay another night, but now the late hour forced them to keep me on in their home. My continued presence and the situation they were put into made them visibly angry. An oppressive silence permeated the room. I did not know what to do. I was shaking inside. Desperate, looking for a way to relieve the tension, I started to clear the table and wash the dishes, but the ladies did not pay attention to what I was doing.

Suddenly, there was a knock at the door and even before Dziunia answered, the big woman, the same one who let me in during the night, entered the room. She was about fifty years old with gray hair pulled back in a small bun at the back of her head. She had a snub nose and narrow piercing eyes in a big, flat face. She approached me surprisingly quickly considering her enormous weight.

"I know that you ladies have a guest. I have been waiting for two days to meet her," she said extending her hand.

"This is Maryla, the daughter of our friends in Warsaw. And this is Helena Kostrzewa, the owner of this house and our closest neighbor," Dziunia introduced us.

I felt her wet hand.

A smile appeared on Helena's face. She gave me a few compliments, adding that she had recognized me as someone from the capital during our first encounter. She wanted to know something about me and learn about life in Warsaw. It was obvious she would have liked to stay longer and chat, but both Slowiks wanted to cut her visit short. Helena asked me how long I would be staying. She explained that if my visit exceeded a few days, she was obliged by the German authorities to register me. Then, expressing hope for a longer conversation in the future, she left the room.

Later, laying in bed, I heard stormy conversations through the closed door. The older lady was talking about the deadly danger brought on them by having a Jewess under their roof. She blamed Dziunia's rashness for keeping me. She was afraid of Helena's and of the other neighbors' snooping. She demanded her daughter force me out of their home the next morning. Dziunia did not disagree with her mother, but she defended her conduct. She said she was personally unable to throw me out into the street where, without their help, I could perish. However, she agreed to let her mother tell me, or do with me, whatever she considered necessary. Their conversation sometimes shifted into a loud quarrel with the older lady crying.

I heard their angry voices late into the night. They were so clear that I had the impression the ladies intended me to hear them. Both women wanted me out of their home immediately, but each of them put the responsibility for telling me on the other. The sentence "YOU tell her to leave our home" was repeated many times by both of them during the course of the night. I was horrified by what was going on behind the door. Only when the voices became silent could I collect my thoughts. I had broken into the quiet life of these women like a storm from a clear sky. I had brought with me the fear of death. I knew how they felt, but I could not do what they wanted. They were the only chance I had. Their home was the first place in which I felt secure since I had escaped from the Ghetto.

I had found two Polish women with warm hearts who understood my ill fortune. Aware of the danger I brought with me, they wanted me out of their life. Still it was difficult for them to tell me to leave their home.

I had come across them through some miraculous coincidence, and now I had to do everything possible to stay with them.

---

(1) Stanislaw was registered as Stanislaw Kostrzewa in the apartment of Helena Kostrzewa at Kilinskiego Street, Number Four in Starachowice.

WAITING FOR THE DOCUMENTS

During a sleepless night, I analyzed my whole situation. I desperately wanted to remain with these nice women and be accepted into their peaceful home. I felt safe and protected here. I considered how to influence their feelings and make them like me. The only way, as I saw it, was always to be pleasant and helpful in every possible way.

I began the implementation of my plan very early the next morning. I knew Dziunia used to make a fire under the kitchen stove and cook breakfast before leaving for work. My first goal was to replace her in this job. I wanted to greet her with a freshly prepared breakfast in a warm kitchen.

The previous evening, I learned where the dried chips and chopped wood were stored. I did not anticipate any problems with this simple chore, however, igniting the fire gave me a lot of trouble. The flame lived only for a short while and neither shielding it with my hands nor blowing air on it seemed to help. I was surprised by my own ignorance and regretted I had not learned the basics of housekeeping at home. As a matter of fact, I couldn't recall a single time when I lit a fire in a furnace. Before the war, there was always a maid in the house. It was her duty to take care of all domestic work. Very seldom was I allowed keeping her company in the kitchen and rarely was I interested in her work. During the war, Sara's mother took upon herself the task of preparing meals for the family. I rarely helped her. As time passed, there was less and less food in the Ghetto and we hardly ever ate a hot meal other than soup. Soup was easy to prepare and easy to divide among all the members of the family. A lot of water and hard to acquire vegetables such as potatoes, carrots, turnips, very often rotten or frozen, were the ingredients of our daily soup.

After we had used up all the wood and coal, the pre-war kitchen oven became useless in the Ghetto. It was replaced by a round, metal oven with a long pipe which ended behind the window. The small surface of the oven served us as a kind of hot plate and the pipe as a heating radiator. During the cold winter months, this oven was the only source of intense, but short-lasting heat for the whole apartment. For a very high price, we could obtain peat or sawdust fuels which were highly contaminated by wet soil. These mixtures were dangerous. They often clogged the airflow and caused explosions, releasing broken pieces of the long pipe and clouds of hot ashes into the air.

Finally, after many unsuccessful tries, I managed to make my first fire in Starachowice. With a hissing sound, the flame enveloped the stacked wood and the whole kitchen started to warm up.

Breakfast was ready and on the table when Dziunia entered the kitchen. The smile on her face was the reward for my troubles. I was glad she invited me to have breakfast with her because the sight of the bread made me very hungry.

Dziunia was in a good mood, talkative, with no trace of the anger and frustration she had shown in the argument with her mother the night before. I felt as if she were radiating cordiality. It was very enjoyable to sit with her at the table. Her warm blue eyes, her lively way of talking, her directness were very pleasant. I felt as if I really were a close friend's daughter just coming for a visit. I liked this feeling. After she left for work, I missed her presence.

Karola Slowik also greeted me in a nice manner and tactfully did not show the dislike and fear she had talked about the previous night. During the day that the two of us spent together, I tried to help her out in everything I could. I was absorbing all the clues about her daily customs and I carefully watched everything she did. I observed how she peeled the vegetables, prepared meals, went about other domestic work and I made mental notes of it all. The older lady was proud of her culinary ability and she gladly shared her knowledge with me.

I familiarized myself with the apartment which consisted of one room, a kitchen and two small, dark attics, one of which served as a bathroom and the other as a storage room. I learned where the items of everyday use were stored. Guided by the hostess, I was allowed to make beds, clean the apartment and help with the cooking. I did the work as well as I possibly could, not sparing myself. At the same time, I tried to smile and keep up an entertaining conversation with the older woman. She was a stickler in everything she did, especially in keeping the apartment in perfect order and sparkling cleanliness. In the evening, she expressed satisfaction with my help, although I still detected a sort of dislike of me under the cover of her politeness.

When both women retired to their room and closed the door, I heard the same stormy conversation I had heard the night before. The mother cried. She demanded Dziunia make me leave. Dziunia agreed I should leave but she wanted her mother to do the job of forcing me out.

A few days passed. During this time I took on heating the oven, preparing simple meals and cleaning the apartment. I constantly volunteered to wash, scrub or polish different objects. Sometimes when I swept the floor, I came across scattered money and once I found a golden broach under the bed. I put all the things I found on the table without comment. I understood my honesty was being tested and this upset me. Before the war, Sara was in the habit of testing a new domestics hired in our home the same way. Maybe for a peasant woman money was of such value that she took the risk and tried to steal it. For me, no money, no golden broach, but the right to sleep in a bed in this home had an indescribable value.

With each passing day, I learned more secrets in the art of cooking. The older lady was a very good teacher. I was a willing and capable student.

apartment. I couldn't allow Dziunia or her mother to carry heavy loads upstairs. I started to bring in wood and coal from the storage shed, water from the well in the backyard and to carry out trash, used water and other waste.

The well had a wooden roller ending in a metal handle. A long rope with a bucket at the end had been wound on the roller. My first attempts to use this simple device were unsuccessful. I was unable to dip the bucket into water and it floated on the surface. While I was fighting with the inertness of the bucket, I heard laughter behind my back. A peasant girl of approximately my age was amused by my clumsiness.

"You are trying to fill the bucket just like a Jewess would," she said. She downed a pail with one single jerk of the rope.

The sound of the word "Jewess" prompted a wave of heat, which like an electric current, passed through my body. However, I smiled and thanked for her help adding that in Warsaw, where I came from, I never saw such a well.

The heated arguments between mother and daughter continued every night without change. Sometimes the exchange of angry words became so loud that I expected the door to open at any moment and to be ordered to remove myself immediately from their home. But nothing like that happened. I was allowed to live the next day as I had the one before in the Slowik's house.

Stanislaw, Dziunia's friend and Helena's cousin, came to us one evening. I was expecting his visit. I already knew he was an active member of an underground political organization and a trusted man. He was about forty years old, of medium build with dark hair and a short moustache. Dziunia openly told him who I was and why I was there. Stanislaw reacted to my story with understanding. He promised to use his underground connections to provide me with authentic documents as soon as possible. In the meantime, I should stay home and avoid walking in the streets. He strongly urged us not to reveal my true identity to any other person, warning us against the neighbors, especially Helena, whose hatred of Jews could become dangerous. "In our house the walls have ears and the tenants are dangerous," he said. Wishing us good luck in these uncertain days of war, he promised to keep in touch.

That night the conversation between the mother and the daughter had a slightly different character. Dziunia wanted me to stay with them for a short time longer only until I received new documents. The older lady's objections were not as vehement as before. This way I learned that I had permission to stay temporarily with the Slowiks. My thankfulness was enormous. Nevertheless, the problem of an unknown future after receiving the documents, depressed me with an even greater force.

I met the other members of the Slowik family during the next few days. Karola Slowik had three children – two daughters and a son. Dziunia, the oldest one, was employed as a cashier in a special store for arms factory workers, where rationed items were sold for very low prices. A cashier had to collect money as well as the ration coupons for all products sold there. Dziunia's salary was small and the assigned food rations did not cover her basic needs. Her total earnings were not sufficient for her two-person household. Dziunia introduced a shrewd method, thanks to which she was able to support not only herself and her mother, but also numerous other people. Her sister's and her brother's families, many friends and acquaintances profited from her help. The supply of food she systematically provided enabled the recipients to live out the long years of war.

The accounts for products sold there were based on the number of coupons. Dziunia cut them out from multi-coupon ration cards in such a way that she obtained proof of selling more food than really took place. For example, she used two halves of one coupon for giving out two full rations. Three small fragments cut from three different coupons and put together were a source for one additional ration. There was a constant fluctuation of personnel, especially the Germans in the arms factory in Starachowice. Their unclaimed rations covered the surplus of food given out. Thanks to Dziunia, it reached many needy people. This kind of coupon manipulation carried a great danger, especially since the control over the store was exclusively in the hands of the Germans. Dziunia knew how much she endangered herself, but the fact that she could help so many people made her brave and gave her fulfillment.

Karola's youngest child was a son named Zdzislaw. He and his wife Stasia and their two-year-old daughter Alinka lived close to his mother. Zdzislaw seldom stayed at home and often disappeared for weeks. When he first came to us, he made an unpleasant impression upon me. He did not look or behave like his sisters or his mother. He was a tall, heavily built, twenty-eight-year-old man with brown hair and dark eyes. His manners were of someone who knows better than anybody else and his way of talking was unusually loud. My presence in his mother's home surprised and also annoyed him. It was obvious he did not believe the story about me being a daughter of a friend from Warsaw. He started to question me, determined to learn the truth. I was not prepared for such a thorough investigation and I had to be very careful with every word.

Stasia, in contrast to her husband, seemed a gentle and tactful person. She came from Kolomyja, a city in southern Poland, where Zdzislaw had been injured during the combat of 1939. He brought Stasia and their child to Starachowice after the outbreak of the Soviet-German war (June of 1941). This whole family was completely supported by Dziunia.

Maria Kamer from Konskie, Karola's middle child, appeared in Starachowice during the first Saturday I was there. At first she didn't associate me with the Jewish girl in the Ghetto to whom she once gave the address of her mother and sister. When she recognized me, she was sincerely surprised to find me there. Late that night, a long and heated conversation between Karola, Dziunia and Maria took place behind the closed door. I learned that Maria had given us her family's address without their permission, and she had neglected to inform them of it subsequently. Sara's arrival had been quite a surprise. However, my appearance at their apartment that night was a completely unexpected blow to them. Now both Karola and Dziunia blamed Maria for putting them in such a difficult and dangerous situation. They accused her of recklessness and lack of responsibility. Maria defended herself, recalling that while in the Konskie Ghetto she was moved by our misery and wanted to encourage us to escape to the Polish side. She did not put much importance to having given us the Slowik address and never imagined we would come to Starachowice.

Maria's arrival gave me a chance to get some information about the fate of the Jews in the Konskie Ghetto. At the beginning of November, Germans and Latvians liquidated almost the whole Ghetto there. The Jewish population of about nine thousand people was transported by freight train from Konskie in an unknown direction. Although Poles were not allowed to approach the Ghetto or the railroad tracks at that time, it was well known that terrible things happened there. Shooting and shouting were heard all over the city for a few days. Only a small number of Jews was left in the Konskie Ghetto after this action.

The following nights my loneliness was especially painful and my longing for the people I had left behind overwhelming. But during the days, I pretended to be content and kept smiling. After all, nobody likes sad and unhappy people, and I tried very hard to be liked by my hostesses. Sometimes, when I couldn't fall asleep, I looked through the window at the bright lights of a distant labor camp where, as I had been told, Jews were imprisoned. A few times, I even saw them being led along the street near our home. I stayed behind the curtains watching them and looking for a familiar face. The Jews, with the Star of David on their clothes, walked slowly, shuffling their feet. Though it was a cold December, no one wore a coat. My heart was with them.

The next day, Maria left with packages of food. She commuted almost every week from Konskie to Starachowice. Dziunia provided food to Maria's family.

Sara and Helenka visited us every few days. Karola always treated them to a meal. I observed with pleasure how politely Helenka behaved at the table. She was reserved, though the food on the table was a big treat for her. She waited for the hostess' invitation and she said thank you for everything. I wondered when and where this child had learned such politeness. Dziunia always gave Sara some food to take along.

Sometimes I saw them off in the evening. We walked along the trails, between the snow-covered fields. Most of the time we did not encounter anybody. I told Sara about the news Maria brought from Konskie. We grieved at the fate of Sara's mother, Izio, my father's assistant, our friends and the whole community we had left behind a few weeks ago. We asked ourselves where could they be now, but we didn't have an answer. I also shared my sad thoughts about my immediate future with Sara. Since I was to receive my new documents soon, I was expecting the Slowik ladies would categorically and openly demand that I leave their home. I would have no choice but to comply with their request. Where would I go? What would I do? Sara was unable to help or advise me. She, herself, was in serious trouble.

I thought for a while about joining the work forces sent to Germany. I could go to the *Arbeitsamt* (1) and volunteer for a job or let myself be caught during a German roundup of Poles in the street. Still, I was afraid that I had only a small chance of surviving as a Pole in a labor camp in Germany. I wouldn't have the possibility of bleaching my hair and the black regrowth would soon give me away as a Jewess. I was thinking more and more about returning to what remained of the Ghetto in Konskie. I knew now there were still some Jews left. I could join them and be among my own people. I knew the Germans intended to make a difficult life for the Jews remaining in Konskie after the liquidation. However, if my life on the Aryan side became impossible, I might have no other choice but to join them and share their fate.

I decided to write a letter to my friend Jack, who probably was still in the Ghetto in Konskie, requesting his advice and help. I planned to ask Maria to deliver my letter to and bring back an answer.

---

(1) Arbeitsamt – German Labor Exchange.

CHRISTMAS

Christmas of 1942 was approaching, bringing great excitement to the Slowik family. Both women impatiently counted the days until the holidays and were completely engrossed in the upcoming family reunion. They expected Maria Kamer and her husband with their daughter from Konskie, Zdzislaw, Stasia and little Alinka to stay with them for at least the last week of December. The previous year, Dziunia's brother and family had not wanted to return to their own home even for the night and slept on straw mattresses on the kitchen floor .

The great preparation, guided by Karola, to which I devoted myself without any restraint, began a few weeks before Christmas. Clean linens for the additional beds, white tablecloth for the holiday celebration and freshly washed curtains for the windows were needed. I started the washing the same way as the professional washerwomen who worked in our home before the war had done it. I put a wooden washtub in the attic in our apartment and filled a big barrel with water from the well. First I soaked the dirty wash in soapy water for twenty-four hours. Next I rubbed each piece on a metal grate. I boiled the white items in a big metal pot, heated on the kitchen stove. The twice-washed laundry was passed through a wringing machine. Then I rinsed it several times in cold water, followed by a rinse in a blue solution. Finally, I starched many pieces in a dense pulp.

I carried the wet linens, tablecloths, curtains, and all the rest of the clean laundry up to the big attic over our building. A narrow ladder led there. I hung everything on the lines to dry. Then Dziunia and I stretched the dried wash which had the fragrance of fresh air. I ironed it on the kitchen table with a red-hot iron. Finally, Karola put all the crisp, folded laundry on the shelves in the closet.

During this whole week of washing, I had carried a

countless number of buckets full of water, wood and coal up and down the stairs. I had worked from the early hours to very late at night, but I didn't spare any effort to do the job well. It gave me a good feeling that Karola and Dziunia needed me and were counting on my help. I felt useful. I was happy when both women praised my work. I did not need any other reward.

A special holiday cleaning of the whole home was the next big job. I washed the windows, doors and scrubbed, waxed and polished the floor. I cleaned all the closets inside and out. I dusted everything, even the glass jars of fruit preserves stored in one of the attics. I noticed that the jars were marked to indicate how much of the contents had already been used. I could not resist tasting these sweet delicacies although I was ashamed of what I was doing. I tried rose-petals fried in sugar, sour cherries, strawberries and green tomatoes. Eating these relishes, I thought about Helenka, who never in her life had tasted something this good. I decided to take a little for her when a chance occurred, and cover my tracks by washing off the old marks and drawing the new levels on the glass containers.

The preparation of holiday meals was the most time-consuming work. Karola was a master cook and she directed, supervised and checked the preparation of each dish. I learned to bake cookies, nougats and layer cakes. I ground sugar with poppy seeds or with yolk until the mixture became smooth, homogeneous butter. I kneaded dough until it left no trace on my hands. I whipped egg whites in the cold air until the fork stood in the hard foam. I crushed dried nuts in the copper mortar. The amount of baked breads and cakes, pickled and smoked meats seemed enormous to me, but Karola was anxious, trusting neither the quantity nor the quality of the prepared food. "The holiday is coming," she kept repeating, trying to justify her anxiety.

Both women tried to take part in these preparations.

Although, Dziunia was very exhausted after a whole day of work in the store, and the physical work was too difficult for Karola, I was always willing to do any kind of work by myself and as well as possible. After a full day of hard work, I fell asleep as soon as my head touched the pillow. Tiredness prevented me from thinking and stifled my fears, which always intensified in every free moment.

I hoped that my complaisance and usefulness, in all situations and at all times, would be noticed and appreciated by Karola. I saw it as the only way to become a well-liked and maybe even irreplaceable part of this family.

I was constantly and insatiably hungry though neither woman spared me food. They always invited me to eat more. I could not restrain myself from eating between meals and late at night. The effect of being well-fed became visible. A healthy, rosy complexion replaced my sallow one. The painful abscesses stopped attacking my body and I began to menstruate after a two-year hiatus. I looked better, healthier and prettier.

One day Dziunia brought home a tall, green tree and put it in the middle of the room. She and her mother decorated the Christmas tree with assorted balls, candles, colorful paper chains, and toys saved from previous years. Then they hung the freshly-made candies and cookies, and finally they sprinkled thin strips of white paper all over the green branches. The gifts for Karola's two granddaughters, were placed under the tree. The Christmas tree looked beautiful and a pleasant smell of the forest permeated the house.

Observing the two women so happy and excited about the coming holidays, I also wanted to feel that way. It was the first Christmas I had experienced so directly and fully. At school there used to be a decorated Christmas tree before the winter break and the students sang carols during the lessons. My Polish classmates awaited Christmas with visible joy and I used to envy them for this and for their glittering trees at home. For me, Christmas meant only that school was closed for the vacation. When I was a child, I felt hurt by fate and angry at not being allowed to have a Christmas tree at home. My parents didn't celebrate any holidays, neither Christian nor Jewish, and I missed all the festivities during my childhood.

Finally the day of Christmas Eve arrived.

Karola started fixing her hair early in the morning. Seeing her difficulties, I offered my help, which she accepted with an obvious lack of confidence in my ability as a hairdresser. I was surprised by my bravado. I had never done anybody's hair. I had never even seen how it was done by a professional hair stylist. Karola's gray hair was thin and delicate as silk. It was hard to shape it. I decided to make it more rigid by covering it with a starch which I cooked for this purpose. Then everything became quite easy. The results of my work came out beyond expectation and Karola's pretty face radiated with happiness. Dziunia immediately became my second client and my   success with her confirmed my recently discovered skill.

The guests from Konskie arrived. Mieczyslaw, Maria's handsome husband, extended his hand to me with a warm smile. Suddenly his expression changed. I saw something resembling horror on his face. I was taken aback by this sudden change and extreme reaction. I couldn't believe that a short look had enabled him to recognize a Jewess in me. Krysia, Maria's seven-year-old daughter, immediately took a dislike to me and was clearly jealous of my presence in her grandmother's home. Zdzislaw, Stasia and Alinka also arrived. It became crowded and loud, but everybody sounded happy. Excitement and the joy of being together were in the air. I was busy helping Karola set the table. Covered with a white tablecloth, decorated with green branches, spread with an assortment of delicious dishes, it looked to me like a royal table.

The Christmas Eve celebration started with the sharing of

the wafer and the expression of good wishes one to another. They all embraced each other and kissed Karola's hand. I followed their example. Christmas Eve supper consisted of twelve meatless dishes, symbolizing – as Dziunia had explained to me – the number of apostles, and lasted for many long hours. The atmosphere at the table was joyous. Everybody was excited by the family gathering and the plentiful, gorgeous food and drink. Karola, surrounded by her children and grandchildren, glowed with happiness. The three siblings, Dziunia, Maria and Zdzislaw, entertained each other with pre-war Christmas memories from their native City of Lodz.

I was very careful all evening to behave as the others did. I shared the wafer, wished everybody Merry Christmas, sang carols I had learned at school, and took part in the conversation. But whatever I did and said, I sensed Mieczyslow's scrutinizing attention. He watched all my movements and listened to everything I said. However, he did not say a word directly to me. His face was serious, although everyone else was laughing and had a good time. I tried to attribute his strange behavior to his personality, but it still made me nervous.

The whole Slowik family agreed to go to the church for Christmas midnight mass. The Germans had suspended the curfew for Christmas Eve. The night was beautiful. The air was crisp and fresh. The sky, covered with innumerable bright stars, looked close to the earth. We walked along the dark roads covered with frozen snow with many people going in the same direction. Men and women, grownups and children, urban and peasant people were passing by and greeted us praising Christ. The church was so full that a crowd had to stay outside in the cold. Luckily, we managed to get in. I took a place close to Dziunia to be able to observe and imitate her. I wet my fingers in the holy water, made the sign of the cross and knelt down on the stone floor as she did.

The organ started to play and the people followed the

melody. There was an outburst of religious emotion in the crowd. The spirit of Christmas, the music, the singing and the special atmosphere in the church united the faithful.

I felt very lonely. I did not belong in this crowd bound by Christianity and Polish nationality. My solitude among strange people, in a strange place and in a strange world, caused me unbearable pain. I missed the people I had grown up with. The ones I had spent my whole life with. I felt, as I never had before, the strong ties with my persecuted nation.

How was it possible that the Polish people were merry when we Jews didn't have a place on earth? Why did they not care that we were perishing? Why were they so indifferent to our suffering? How would the crowd gathered in this church react if I publicly confessed to being a Jewess?

The holidays passed without any disturbance. During this time I managed to overcome Krysia's dislike of me by making up bedtime stories. But I was unable to break through the wall separating Mieczyslaw from me. All my attempts to have some contact with him failed.

Many people visited the Slowiks with holiday wishes. I had to meet them all because there was no way I could avoid them in our small apartment. I met the tenants of our and the adjoining buildings, Dziunias's friends from work and Karola's acquaintances. The constant public exposure, my scrutiny of each said word, the stories I had to invent for every visitor exhausted me more than the physical work.

One night I wrote a short letter to my friend, Jack (Jakub Lejbusiewicz), who had stayed in the Ghetto when I escaped. It was written in such a way that a stranger would see it as a note about the health, vacation plans and the various affairs of my family. However, Jack would understand it quite differently. He would learn my situation on the Aryan side was so difficult that I was considering a return to the Konskie Ghetto. I also asked him about his family and the present life in the Ghetto.

When I found myself alone with Maria, I asked her to deliver my letter to Jack in Konskie. I openly explained why I was asking her for this favor. Maria not only agreed, but also promised to bring the answer during her next visit to Starachowice. She felt sorry that I was thinking about returning to the Ghetto. It seemed to me that she really understood the hopelessness of my situation.

Taking the opportunity of being alone with her, I asked if she had noticed her husband's strange behavior toward me. Maria had not only noticed it, but she wanted to talk about it when time permitted.

One evening Maria invited me for a walk. When we moved away from home and reached a path in an empty field, she explained Mieczyslaw's strange reaction when he first met me. It was a big surprise to me.

In the early summer of 1942 in Konskie, Mieczyslaw saw a group of young women escorted by Jewish policemen. Each of them wore a white band with the blue Star of David on her right arm. The appearance of the Jewish girls on a quiet, suburban street at that time made him curious. After that, hiding behind a curtain in his home or a tree in the garden, he regularly watched the passing female squad each morning and each evening. After some time, he got so familiar with the women that he was able to identify each individual. He took a special interest in one girl whom he called the "Black Jewess". She was easily noticeable because she always wore a black dress. Her braids, as dark as her clothes, were tied at the back of her head. In time, he even developed a kind of warm feeling for this Jewess. He would have liked to have known something about her, to at least learn her name, but he was afraid to ask about someone from the Ghetto.

During the following weeks, he found out the group of Jewish girls worked in a pre-war high school building on Polna Street, converted to a special school for Young Nazis at that time. A few months passed. One day in the fall of 1942, the Jewesses stopped appearing on Polna Street. Mieczyslaw missed the sight of them, especially of the Black one, and he often wondered about her fate. However, he kept his secret and confessed to no one, not even his wife, that he had become interested in a girl from the Ghetto.

According to his personal philosophy, the only Poles who would likely survive the war were those who could remain aloof and unnoticed to the occupying force. He believed Polish people should comply with German orders and do nothing forbidden if at all possible. The fact that he had observed the Jewish girls and even had developed a fondness for them was contradictory to German rules and dangerous to him.

Already at the beginning of the war, the Kamer family was expelled from their apartment in Lodz. The Germans confiscated almost everything they owned and ordered them to leave the city in a very short time. Mieczyslaw moved his family to Konskie, where he purposely rented a place on the outskirts of the town. He did not want to work for the Germans and left home only reluctantly.

Mieczyslaw had agreed to spend Christmas at this mother-in-law's home for the first time that year, yielding to Maria's and Krysia's persuasions. He was surprised to find a stranger there and was shocked by my similarity to the "Black Jewess". During the first few hours he spent with me, his initial suspicion turned to conviction that I was the Jewish girl he had observed in Konskie.

The presence of a Jewess in his family home so terrified him that he confessed to Maria his platonic obsession during the past summer. Although my blond hair confused him at the first, he later became convinced that I was the "Black Jewess" from Konskie and not a daughter of his mother-in-law's old friend from Warsaw. He wanted to leave Dziunia's home immediately and return to Konskie. Begged by the whole family, he agreed to stay until the end of the holiday. He threatened never to come again if I were to stay in Starachowice.

I believed that Mieczyslaw had correctly identified me as the "Black Jewess" from his story. I did work in the school for the Young Nazis in Konskie for several months. I was being escorted in a group of girls by Jewish policemen on the way there. My daily route was along Polna Street, where the Kamer family lived. I always wore a black dress as a way of expressing mourning after my father's recent death. And I tied my black braids at the back of my head.

Walking in the middle of the street, I tried not to look at the Poles watching us from the sidewalks. Often, I heard passersby's mocking us quite often. I was humiliated by the fact that I was escorted by policemen like a criminal, that I was marked by a white band on my arm, that I was not allowed to walk on the sidewalk, that I had to yield to everyone, that I was imprisoned in the Ghetto. I was humiliated by being a Jewess. I tried to walk with my eyes down and avoid any eye contact with my old Polish acquaintances. No wonder I never noticed Mieczyslaw. I saw him for the first time in my life at Dziunia's apartment on Christmas Eve.

The chain of these strange coincidences worried me. I was afraid of the disagreement it would cause among the members of the Slowik family. Luckily, Mieczyslaw's sensational story had not make an impression on Maria.

"Don't worry, he is chicken-hearted." She dismissed the whole tale with a short statement.

I could not sleep during the following night. The recollections of my work in the Hitler Youth School came back to me very clearly. It was only a few months ago, although I felt as if years had passed.

At the beginning of June of 1942, news started circulating in the Ghetto that the Gestapo, bribed by some rich Jews, had created a special job for women in the Young Nazis School. Until then, there had been no work for females in the Konskie Ghetto except for a few in the sewing shop. All the positions in the Jewish Council, in all the different committees and subcommittees, in the police department, in the sanitary and health services and in the working brigades were reserved for men. It was believed that a document proving employment by or for the Germans protected one from deportation from Konskie. It was considered the guarantee of safety by the Jews. Women did not have such protection. Thus they, like all old people and children, were constantly in danger of being sent away.

When my father, already very weak and confined to bed, heard about this "remarkable" opportunity for young women, he told me that, "It would be very good if you could be accepted for this work".

However, I did not apply for this job because I simply did not believe I would be hired.

A few days after his death, a policeman brought a letter from the Jewish Council (*Judenrat*) ordering me to appear in their office. Such a letter could mean danger. Many times, the Jewish Council had summoned people to their headquarters and the Germans had transported them immediately to faraway camps. The deportation was so organized that the Jews who were caught didn't even have a chance to notify their families.

The policeman who escorted me to the Council understood my terror. He reassured me that the Germans were not demanding people for deportation that day. To my surprise, Rosen, the chairman of the Jewish Council of the Konskie Ghetto, asked me into his office. He informed me that, thanks to my father's life-long social work for the Jewish community, the Council was including me in a special group of girls who would be employed in the school for Young Nazis. He told me that I should obey all the orders and submit myself to the strict discipline there. He cautioned me about disobedience, no matter how small, which could cause a deadly consequence to the entire group.

In this way, I found myself among the young women who, received a German guarantee to be left safely in our Ghetto. The building of the pre-war Saint Stanislaw Kostka's High School, Number 333, where I had graduated from the third grade before the war, was my place of work. The German students were on vacation during the summer months and the school administration was preparing this facility for their return.

Approximately thirty Jewish women from the ages of sixteen

to twenty-five were assigned to this job. I knew all these girls well and had even attended school with some of them. They came mostly from wealthy families. They were daughters of the owners of factories, big shops and houses. The fact that the rich girls were employed in this job seemed to confirm a rumor that the Germans had been bribed.

The Jewish policemen escorted us to work early in the morning. We were then divided into small working groups with a Polish or German woman in charge. A Polish woman, who had been a janitor in the pre-war high school, was in charge of the group to which I was assigned. She had known me well in the old days. Twice a day, I had been in her home during the three years preceding the war. Together, with a few other students, I had stored my coat in her closet. The janitor received a monthly payment from our parents for this service.

She recognized me immediately and greeted me with malicious satisfaction, shouting abusive words, as if it were I who had caused her pre-war poverty. It seemed that her present social rise and the Jews' degradation created a special kind of cruelty in her. Calling me the worst anti-Semitic names, she ordered me to clean the toilets. The school toilets were in a separate small building. They were primitive, dirty and stank from far away. The toilet cleaning disgusted me so much that I fought nausea all the time. While working there, I unexpectedly lost consciousness and fell down. When I awakened, I was lying on the grass in the courtyard. The girls I worked with had applied a wet rag to my injured head. That day, we all felt so sick that no girl from my group could eat the soup at noon although we had not eaten for many hours. After a short break, we returned to the toilet cleaning. The janitor continued to abuse us, especially me, with dirty words and the threat of beatings. The policemen took us back to the ghetto late in the evening.

This was the "ideal job" I was lucky to get, making me the subject of envy of many not-so-fortunate young women in the

Ghetto. The presumed protection from deportation added a high value to this job. The subhuman working conditions and the lack of any pay did not seem to be so important in this case.

A few weeks elapsed. During this time, I washed the toilets and spread manure in the garden from the very early morning until late in the evening. Then, one day, I happened to notice something unusual about the hands of a Polish girl who brought us our bucket of daily soup. I recalled reading, a long time ago, an Egyptian dream-book with a description of palm-reading. I decided to use this opportunity and asked the girl if she would like to know her future. She grew excited and her facial expressions greatly aided my palmistry. Most of the time, I knew what she wanted to hear, but when my foretelling could be checked easily and quickly I gave her enigmatic answers.

From that time on, my reputation as the fortune-teller became famous among Polish workers in the kitchen. I started to have more and more "clients" and received food as payment from some of them. Thanks to the recommendation of these women to the German office, I was transferred to work in the kitchen. My working condition improved radically. Though I still slaved twelve long hours a day, peeling potatoes and vegetables, scrubbing dishes and floors, I had a better supervisor and best of all, more food than before. Unfortunately, I did not stay in the kitchen long . I was constantly moved to other jobs. At one time, I was assigned to the ironing group. I ironed men's shirts, women's uniforms, linen and other items with a hot iron, standing all day long. A young German female guard kept snapping a riding-whip each time she noticed a wrinkled piece. Terrified by the hissing sound of her whip, I could hardly hold the hot iron. Later I worked in the fields and in the garden, harvesting vegetables and fruits. The advantage of this particular job was that I could sometimes smuggle an apple or a tomato for Helenka. I was also assigned to a group washing the windows and it was again the janitor who was in charge of it. The school building was three floors high and there were many tall double windows. They all opened to the outside and were accessible for washing only from the edge of the narrow windowsill. There were no handles to hold on to. The janitor was always watching our work and abusing us with vulgar words, but her anger and hatred were mostly directed toward me. One day I was washing the outside glass of a window on the third floor, standing on the windowsill, leaning out. The janitor started to beat me on my legs with a dripping wet rag. To keep myself from losing my balance, I tried to push my body inside the room. The infuriated janitor intensified the beating, hitting me on my face. Soaked, I stayed in the open window on the narrow windowsill, high in the air, blinded by the painful blows. The janitor was much older than I and probably weaker. I felt a strong desire to grab her rag and strike back but I could imagine the consequences of this for me and also for the other girls. Covering my face against the blows, I swore vengeance. This allowed me to take all the humiliating slaps in my face (1).

In September of 1942 this "miracle job", which was supposed to safeguard us, ceased to exist. I ran away from the Ghetto a short time thereafter.

---

(1) After I was liberated in January, 1945, I went to Konskie to fulfill the pledge of vengeance I had made to myself in 1942. I easily found the janitor, who still lived in her old apartment on the premises of the pre-war high school. She recognized me immediately. Seeing me alive in front of her, she came to a standstill. I ordered her to bring a rag and a bucket of water. Holding a wet rag in my hand, I told her that I was going to beat her the same way she had beaten me three years before. I was determined to do it. I had come one hundred miles especially to do it. I was convinced that I could . But then I saw an old woman shaking from fear in front of me. I could not hit her. I left and never saw her again.

END OF THE GHETTO IN KONSKIE

The Christmas holidays ended. The Kamers returned to Konskie and Zdzislaw's family moved back to their apartment in Starachowice. Dziunia continued her daily work in the store of the munitions factory. It was January, 1943.

After the departure of the guests, the rhythm of our life returned to the pre-holiday routine. Now after weeks of intensive practice, I could do all the housework much more easily. I already knew how to prepare breakfasts, lunches, dinners, bake a variety of different cakes and cook many complicated dishes. I was familiar with everything in the apartment and knew when and what to clean, dust, polish and wash. Most importantly, I learned more about both women's characters and customs. That allowed me to please them in many different ways. Karola, who in the past had supervised all my work now, gave me much more independence. She sometimes loudly admitted that, thanks to my help, she was not so tired anymore and had time to enjoy her family.

Karola very much liked that late hour of the day, when twilight was replaced by the darkness of the night. She made me rest during this special time. I had to stop whatever I was doing and we both took our places around the warm kitchen oven. The last rays of the day were coming through the window painted with frost. In dusk, I could see that Karola prayed, moving her rosary beads. At this hour, given by her to God, she felt His protective closeness.

The wind had been very strong these last few weeks. Our home on the hill was subjected to its violent power. The loud blowing always sounded like a cry for help. Especially at twilight, when complete silence reigned in our apartment, the wailing of the wind was very distressing to me.

At such times, I had the clear feeling that the walls of this apartment guarded me against the Germans, that only here I could be safe. My closeness to the praying woman also added an element of mystical protection.

I had not received any religious upbringing at home. My parents had openly demonstrated their atheism. Early in my life, I had taken from them and from my closest surroundings the ironical, even aggressive, approach to all religions, including Judaism.

But now, when I was always afraid of losing the roof over my head, of everyone suspicious, of people's hate toward Jews, I wanted to believe in God. I wanted to pray for His mercy. I wanted to have confidence in His protective power over my fate. I wanted to beg Him to help me, calm my fear and guide me to my rescue. I thought that if I knew how to ask God with all my heart, I would get the needed guidance.

Both Slowik women were devout Catholics. They prayed every day, attended Sunday sermons in church and often received Holy Communion. They deeply loved the Holy Mother and her Child Jesus. They referred to them as they would to close, well known, dear people. Grateful for all the good things in their lives, they attributed their luck to heavenly intervention. They trusted in an ultimate justice, even if the ways of Providence were not always understood by them. Very often, the inner peace, which radiated from their deep religious faith, nourished me and soothed my fear.

Karola had "weak eyes" and glasses did not help her see well. After I had heard her complaints that she had lost the pleasure of books with the loss of sight, I started to read to her. Every evening, when the full darkness had filled the kitchen, we turned on the light and I read different novels out loud. Karola liked it and looked forward to these evening moments. According to her, the intonation of my voice brought to life the heroes of the stories and their lives became real. Thanks to my reading, she was able to enjoy the fictional world described in the books.

Pleasing her made me happy. I hoped that the time we spent together reading would bring me closer to her. I wished that this way she would get used to me and even would start to like my presence in her home.

However, I could still hear conversations between the mother and the daughter about me. Both of them invariably wanted me out of their home. They impatiently waited for the moment when I would receive the documents from Stanislaw. Yet I had an impression that the talks about me were less frequent and not so dramatic.

I waited impatiently for Maria's return. Often in the hour of dusk, my thoughts went to my friends trapped in the Ghetto or in unknown labor camps. How could they manage to exist in such cold weather, constantly hungry, attacked by disease. I was unable to imagine their lives. The fact that even in my daydreams I couldn't reach them and be with them made me very lonely. I thought about returning to the Ghetto in Konskie more and more often.

Maria arrived one day and brought the letter I had been waiting for. It was a small square piece of paper with a few words written with blue pencil, "*Halina komme, sofort, aber noch heute Jack*" which means: "Halina, come immediately, even today Jack." My name was underlined with a straight line.

Maria described how she had contacted Jack. One day, walking along the fence dividing the Polish part of Krakowska Street from the Ghetto, she noticed a Jewish girl on the other side. Then Maria whispered my name a few times. The girl approached the fence and asked about me. It became clear from her questions that she had known me well and was interested in my present fate. Maria gave her the letter for Jack.

She returned to the same place at the same time the following day. Jack waited for her at the fence. The conversation between them was very short. Jack was under the impression that I had not left Konskie and was still hidden some place in this city. He insisted on my immediate return to the Ghetto. Maria promised to deliver his message to me as soon as possible, but she did not inform him about my whereabouts.

Jack's letter made a strong impression on me. On the one hand, it confirmed that my old world really had existed, which I had already started to doubt. It also proved to me that Jack was in good health and wanted me to come back. On the other hand, this short note surprised me by its complete lack of answers to my questions. He did not convey any information about his life, his six siblings and his parents. He did not mention the place where the people from the Konskie Ghetto had been taken.

Looking at the small piece of paper held by Jack a day before, I saw a caution in its seven-word message. I recalled my own arguments which, at the end of October of last year, had forced me to leave everybody and run away from the Ghetto. Again, I felt the grip of danger surrounding me. I felt intense fear and its bitter taste.

Karola and Dziunia did not comment on Jack's letter. They retired, leaving me alone with my thoughts. I couldn't detach myself from this scrap of paper. I kept reading the short note over and over again, "Halina, come immediately, even today ..."

I wrote the second letter to Jack that night. I asked him for an explanation of some very important problems. I wanted to know his answer before rushing back to the Ghetto. My decision depended on Jack's reply. The letter was short and written in such a way that it did not present danger to the messenger. Maria agreed to smuggle my new note to Jack.

After about ten days, Maria was back in her mother's home. This time she brought no letter for me. She did not meet the Jewish girl at the other side of the fence. She did not see Jack or any other Jew. The Ghetto in Konskie had ceased to exist. The Germans deported all the Jews left there after the November action. They conducted their deportation fast and in a quiet way. Maria learned that Konskie had become a Jew-free city, but she was unable to find out where the Jews had been sent (1).

About 9,000 Jews from Konskie, who had been present in this Ghetto at the end of October, 1942, vanished. Among them were approximately 6,500 Jewish inhabitants of the pre-war City of Konskie (half of its total population), Jews deported from many surrounding small communities, and Jews expelled from the City of Lodz. The people among whom I had been born and lived for 18 years, my friends, colleagues, neighbors, acquaintances, aunt Miriam Szpitbaum, Jakub (Jack) Lejbusiewicz from Essen vanished into thin air (2). My world, the only one I knew, did not exist anymore.

A few days had passed when one evening Dziunia embraced and kissed me. I was surprised by her sudden and unexpected show of affection. She had never done it before. Karola left the room at this moment, as if on an agreed-upon sign. I realized that I would hear something very important when we two were alone. I dreaded this inevitable news.

Dziunia told me the Germans had transported Jews from all the ghettos to the death camps. Such places of extermination were in Oswiecim (*Auschwitz*) and Treblinka. The Jews first had been packed into closed freight trains where many people died from lack of air, food and water during the long trip. Those people who survived this journey were then poisoned by gas in the special chambers and their bodies burned in the ovens. A dark smoke covered the sky around these places. The stench of burning bodies saturated the air in a large radius from these death camps.

I listened to this story with complete disbelief. I was even surprised that Dziunia could uncritically believe such improbable news. When I asked her for the source of this information, she gave me a meaningless answer, as if this was generally well known. I became angry with Dziunia. I did not understand how such a good, honest woman could repeat this

125

anti-Semitic nonsense. What should I expect from the people who did not have her unusual qualities?

I recalled a tale very popular among the Polish population that Jews had added Christian children's blood to the production of matzo. Though this story was different, I saw an analogy between the accusation of Jews of ritual murder and the theory of gassing people in a death camp. To me, the name of the similarity was anti-Semitism.

Dziunia didn't even try to convince me her news was true. She left me alone with this terrible information and did not mention it again. The next day, I repeated everything to Sara. Her reaction was the same as mine. She did not believe such perfidious crime was possible.

During the following days, I couldn't forget even for a minute about the death camps. With the passing of time, this information, initially unbelievable, became more and more probable. I started to understand why the Jews who were deported from the Ghetto had not sent any sign of their existence. The names of the Cities Oswiecim and Treblinka became imprinted in my mind.

---

(1) In January of 1943, approximately 300 Jews, who had been left in the Ghetto in Konskie after the first liquidation in November, 1942, were transported to Szydlowiec and then to the place of their death in Treblinka. (Bulletin of Jewish Historic Institute in Warsaw, Poland; #15-1.s 78, 8491, 151, 17).

(2) After the war, I estimated only about a dozen people from the Ghetto in Konskie survived the war. I, Sara and Helenka were a big fraction of this number.

One evening Stanislaw appeared in our apartment. His face radiated with happiness when he handed me the promised official papers. It was a birth certificate issued by a Roman Catholic parish stating on January 23, 1923 a daughter born to Katarzyna and Jan Czajkowski in Kolonie Konarskie, District Opatow, Province Kielce, was baptized Jozefa. The newborn baby girl had died and her death had been noted in the archives of the church. However, thanks to Stanislaw's intervention, the certificate of death had been destroyed and Jozefa was alive according to the official documentation of the parish. I became now the continuation of her short existence in this world.

Both Slowik women decided that they would continue to call me Maryla because neither they nor I particularly liked the name Jozefa.

Stanislaw also brought the official note from the town of Kolonie Konarskie, that Jozefa Czajkowska was a resident there until a few days ago. He wanted me to be registered in Starachowice as soon as possible. First of all this was necessary for the safety of the people who were involved in arranging my documents. Besides it would also satisfy Helena who had constantly complained about my stay in her house without formal registration, which could cause dangerous consequences for her.

The new papers, and even more, the necessity of the quick official registration in Starachowice, excited me but only for a short time. Soon I was terrified by a new thought. I remembered well the frequent nightly conversations between Dziunia and her mother. I was afraid now of being forced to leave the Slowik's home since I already had the documents. I held the precious papers fearing what would await me in the next moment.

Meantime, Stanislaw was talking about the recent political news and his words interrupted the flow of my unpleasant associations. English radio announced the enormous German Army, under the command of Paulus, had been surrounded in the City of Stalingrad in the Soviet Union. The Allied commanders estimated the Russians would liquidate or imprison several hundred thousand encircled German soldiers in the very near future. The German defeat was of such magnitude that it could be compared only to Napoleon's defeat near Moscow in 1812. The Germans were also met with repulses in Africa. The Allies, including the newly arrived American battalions, were conquering the German Army, under the command of Rommel, pushing them out of Africa.

According to Stanislaw's optimistic opinion, the general political situation was very good. The victory of the Allies over the Germans was indisputable and the final German defeat should come no later than spring, 1943.

I got intoxicated from this wonderful information. During the past years, I did not have a chance to hear the truthful news. The political reports, given to us from German propaganda, were always filled with their successes toward the ultimate enslavement of Europe. Enclosed in the Ghetto, I was completely deprived of the news broadcasting from London. The Germans had ordered the Jews to relinquish all their radios at the very beginning of the war. The punishment for not complying with German instruction was, as always, death. In the overcrowded Ghetto where there was a complete lack of space, no one had any ability to hide them effectively.

All the information we heard was based on word of mouth transmission that "somebody heard it from somebody who heard it from somebody else". The credibility of this kind of news was problematic. Usually, it contained information not reflecting the truth, but rather helping us to survive by lifting our spirits. The attention in the Ghetto was focused on constant danger and the difficulties of everyday life. What happened far away from us was less important than what was going on directly in our streets and courtyards.

Listening to the magnificent successes of the Allies, I felt alive again. Perhaps only a couple of months separated me from the end of the war. A new hope was born. For certain, Dziunia and her mother would let me stay with them through this short time. They wouldn't have the heart to order me out into the icy streets, full of Germans, when the end of the war was so near.

The sound of our joy crossed the thin walls and Helena, curious, came in to find its reason. Hearing the good news, she joined us in a celebration of the approaching German defeat.

Helena had shown her great patriotism often. She had imagined a free post-war Poland, nationally and religiously homogeneous. In her liberated homeland, there was no place for any minorities, especially Jews, whom she hated with all her heart. She expressed this political view freely and without any special precaution. I had a chance to observe it during the holidays when she had talked to complete strangers in our home. Helena visited the Slowiks frequently and almost always switched the subject of conversation to the Jews. Listening to her dirty, anti-Semitic epithets, I felt as if a wave of heat covered my body and face. My cheeks became visibly red. It took all my willpower to control these symptoms. Sometimes I could succeed. Most of the time, I had to use many different tricks to cover my strange reaction to her assaults on Jews.

Helena never could get Karola's support in her anti-Semitic attitude. Therefore, she often looked for my approval and appreciation. In such a situation, I pretended to be busy with some urgent work, but when it was impossible I behaved as if I were bored with the Jewish topic. I never was brave enough to openly defend Jews. Though I knew that my behavior was motivated by safety, I later felt as if I had betrayed a close friend.

A few days later, Dziunia formally registered me in the office of Starachowice. She showed me and her mother the registration book, usually kept by Helena Kostrzewa, the owner of the house at Kilinskiego, Number Four, in Starachowice. Now, in the Slowik's apartment the name of Jozefa Czajkowska also appeared. "The cousin of Karolina Slowik" was written in the space provided for the information about the relationship to the head of the household.

Dziuna explained since I was going to officially live with them, making me a member of her family was safer for everybody. To my surprise, Karola did not express any objection. Later that day, she asked me to call her "aunt".

Helena, however, came to us immediately demanding an explanation of all the discrepancies with regard to my personal data. She remembered that when I appeared at the door of her house, I introduced myself as Maria Nowakowska. Now I was claiming to be Jozefa Czajkowska. She suspected some important secret was hidden in that and was hurt by not being trusted with it.

Dziunia explained this discrepancy, telling an invented but at the same time probable story. According to it, the Germans had caught me on a street of Warsaw and sent me to Germany to work. I was lucky to escape from the train during the trip. However, being now on the German list of escapees, I could not return to my home in Warsaw. My mother had advised me to take refuge in Starachowice with Karolina Slowik, her school friend. That first night, when Helena questioned me through the closed door, I gave her, an unknown person, a false name. In fact, my last name was Czajkowska and the first one Jozefa, though my parents always had called me Maryla. By now, my case was probably forgotten by the Germans and my official registration in Starachowice became possible.

Helena accepted this explanation with total confidence and promised to keep this information to herself. The fact that she was included in my private secret visibly improved her relationship with me. Now, the document, the formal registration in the Slowik's home and the friendship with the owner of their house made me finally feel secure.

One day Karola decided to go with me to the local market to shop for some needed products. This marketplace was situated in the middle of the city at some distance from our house. It was a cold and windy day. In such weather the long trip could be difficult for an elderly lady. To be of help to her, I volunteered to go there alone.

I ventured downtown seldom and very reluctantly. Starachowice was situated not far from Konskie. The munitions factory there employed many people commuting from different cities. There was a large probability that somebody who remembered me from school or from the streets of Konskie would recognize me.

I walked fast on the empty streets, seldom passing anyone. I was warmly dressed. I wore Dziunia's woolen shawl protecting my head and almost my whole face from the cold wind. My blond hair was purposely visible under the shawl.

I found the marketplace without difficulty. There were very few people there. Several urban-looking women were buying from the peasants' carts. A small group of people talked in the middle of the lot. I went first through the whole marketplace, walking from one cart to another, looking for the best products at the lowest prices. When I found them, I bought them rather quickly. When I paid for the last purchase, I heard a loud scream. The clear words of this cry went through me like a bullet from a gun, "A Jewess, people look, there is a Jewess!"

I immediately turned and looked in the direction of the voice. A teenage boy stood a small distance from me. He looked straight at me. His extended hand pointed at me. His accusation was directed toward me. His face was filled with joy. His playful mood was because of me. He had discovered my deadly secret and he amused himself with this revelation.

The loud scream, "A Jewess, people look, there is a Jewess!" heard in the whole market, terrified me enormously. At the same time the boy's joyous face made me very angry.

This shrewd youth suddenly endangered me and maybe also Dziunia's and Karola's lives by his malicious pleasure. I flew into a rage.

As quickly as I could, I jumped at the boy who still stood with his extended hand in my direction. I grabbed him by the lapels of his garment and pushed him with a fury. I shouted straight in his face so loudly that everybody in the marketplace could hear me, "Damn it. Where is this rotten Jewess? Don't let her run away. Get her fast."

I kept repeating the same sentence many times, changing curses and anti-Jewish epithets, demonstrating knowledge of the rich, dirty Polish vocabulary as well as a profound hate for the Jews.

My aggressiveness and my anger completely surprised the boy. Stupefied, he was unable to utter a word. He tried to get out of my grip, but I held onto him. I imagined that as long as I could keep him in my hands, I could also control him and force him to call off his public accusation. I angrily demanded a response from him as if catching this Jewess was solely my duty. I kept pushing him and shouting at him. Finally, the terrified boy admitted he had not seen any Jewess in the marketplace. His stuttered words were loud and clear. Still holding onto him, I turned to see the public reaction. The people were standing in the same places as before, but they were all looking at us. Nobody said anything. Silence ruled over the marketplace.

"It is a pity that no Jewess was here," I said to the boy, loosening my grip. "Your father should teach you a lesson for this stupid game you wanted to play with the grownups."

The boy disappeared so fast that I was unable to notice in which direction he took off.

I arranged the shawl on my head and very slowly left the market. Once on the street again, I sped up and soon turned into the first path leading through the fields. I walked fast looking straight ahead of me. Not until I was some distance from the marketplace did I stop and turn around. The whole visible space was empty. I was alone in the snow-covered field. Nobody was following me.

Only then did the reaction to the recent incident overwhelm me. My knees buckled as if they couldn't keep my body in a vertical position any longer. My shaking hands were unable to hold the basket and the products scattered on the snow. I shivered and felt nauseated. I crouched on the ground trying to overcome the trembling of my hands, the weakness of my legs and the nausea.

It took some time for all these symptoms to disappear and then I was able to concentrate on what had happened.

I recalled the small boy, hardly reaching to my shoulder, who was the cause of this terrifying episode. He had been wearing an oversized jacket, too thin for a cold day, a brown, handmade woolen shawl around his neck and a cap on his head. He was a poor youth, without a warm coat for the winter season. He was from the city not from the countryside, as his dialect indicated. I knew he was alone in the marketplace because nobody came to his rescue when I pushed and shook him.

How was it possible that this common boy recognized a Jewish girl in me? I was making my purchases fast, choosing the proper products and moving from one cart to another. I was preoccupied with what I was doing. I did not think about any danger. How did he see the Jewess in me? What differentiated me from all the other people gathered at the marketplace?

It must have been something in me which gave me away. It had to be a moment when he was so close to me that he could look into my eyes. Maybe there he saw the look of a hunted person. These few seconds were sufficient for him to discover my deadly secret.

This malicious boy's accusation could cause a situation when even the most "perfect" documents wouldn't save me.

His public statement could leave me no time to defend myself. It could also create deadly consequences for the Slowik family.

Jozefa Czajkowska's papers protected me when I was not suspected of being a Jewess. But in the face of such an accusation, the so-called "good papers" were without value. During a thorough police investigation my false identity wouldn't be difficult to discover. I wondered about the final ending of this episode if my reaction had been different. What would be my fate if a German or a Polish policeman had been present at that time in the marketplace?

I realized that even with my new papers, danger threatened me at every moment, everywhere, from everyone.

I had to go back home. I was afraid Karola would start worrying about my long absence. I put together the products scattered on the ground and went in the direction of home. The fast walk uphill took away my breath but simultaneously restored my lost calm.

I decided that the incident at the marketplace would remain my secret.

Sara, with Helenka, left Starachowice in the spring of 1943. She had been unable to find a paying job during their time in this city. The financial resources she had brought from the Ghetto were almost gone, although she tried to keep their expenses to a minimum. Sara and Helenka spent many days of the long winter of 1942 / 1943 in bed in their dark and cold room. They were often hungry. Dziunia tried to help them. Whenever possible she arranged food supplies for Sara from the store where she worked. However, taking her own and Sara's safety into consideration, she was unable to do it often. Karola also helped by inviting them for occasional meals. Usually after such a visit Sara went home with a package of food..

However, Karola had to limit her contact with Sara because of Helena's curiosity. Our landlady was interested in all our guests, but especially in Sara and Helenka. Helena was always waiting for their arrival. Whenever she heard a child's footsteps on the stairs, she immediately came out of her apartment and showered our visitors with questions. This caused Sara and Helenka anxiety and even fear.

From the first day, Sara had problems with the people where she was living. Over time, her landlady became openly hostile. Finally, she ordered Sara to vacate the rented room as soon as possible. When staying there became impossible, Stanislaw helped her again. He found Sara and Helena a place to live through his best friend Peter. It was in a small town, east of Starachowice, at the east side of the Vistula River. Stanislaw was convinced that Sara could find food and shelter as payment for helping on the farm. He even prepared Sara for a life among peasants so she would know how to generate confidence instead of dangerous suspicions. He had knowledge of the peasants' mentality and their customs as if he had spent a big part of his life among them.

One evening I said goodbye to Sara and Helenka on the path between the fields. Although I saw them quite seldom and never visited them in their home, the knowledge of their presence nearby was a comfort to me. Now we were going to be separated for an unspecified length of time. For safety reasons, we decided not to correspond or communicate in any way. The next meeting, according to our plans, would take place in the Slowik home after the war.

Their departure was painful to me. Extreme loneliness overwhelmed me. I could not rid myself of the feeling that Sara and Helenka were leaving me forever.

I met Stanislaw infrequently. He would disappear for several weeks and then unexpectedly reappear in Helena's apartment which he called his home. I had already learned he was a liaison officer and an activist in the underground army of GL (Gwardia Ludowa – People's Guard) (1). After each absence, he used to come to the Slowiks for a long talk. He always knew the current news from the English radio or from the illegal newspapers. He was our main source of information. Thanks to him we learned about the international and national political events and even about the local news. I no longer had any doubt about the Jews' deadly fate. I constantly learned about more places of their slaughter.

One day I heard about the Jewish uprising in Warsaw. Stanislaw told us two flags, one white/red, the second one white with the Star of David, fluttered side by side above the Warsaw Ghetto during the uprising. He was excited by the open display of Polish statehood by Jews. He praised them for that. He was fascinated by the heroism of the people fighting in the streets of the Warsaw Ghetto.

The thought of the Warsaw Jews dying in an uneven fight, being trapped in the streets, burned alive within the walls of their homes, gassed in the underground passages, did not elicit any pride in me. On the contrary, it upset me. I heard the painful cry for help in their hopeless uprising against the well-armed Germans. I knew all the fighters were condemned to die, just as all the Jews in Poland. I did not hope for any help from Poles. I foresaw their lonely death in an indifferent and hostile world. I felt the heavy weight of this knowledge locked inside me, hidden from the eyes of others.

Helena and the neighbors, whom I used to meet in the courtyard, and other people who were visiting Karola, made jokes about the Jewish fighters. Imitating the Jewish accent, they mocked their courage and laughed at their tragedy.

Dzunia and her mother were convinced that the end of the war would come in a very short time. That stimulated their patriotic feelings. They wanted to be more active in the resistance against the Germans. Our home became the contact place for AK (Armia Krajowa – Home Army) (2) an illegal Polish organization. Quite often, we stored secret papers, huge amounts of dried crackers, men's clothing and even guns. We didn't have any proper place to hide these items, possession of which the Germans penalized by death. We covered them with old blankets in the storage area adjacent to the bedroom. The members of the AK city unit and the partisans, the members from the forest, visited us often. Our house at the edge of town was relatively easy to reach. Sometimes during the night, we were awakened by the gentle sound of clods of earth being thrown against the window. I could then see the silhouette of a man in the darkness of the night. Very quietly, trying not to wake the neighbors, we let the "forest boys" in.

They were all emaciated, tired and dirty young men. They could seldom rest, wash themselves or eat. Most of the time, they took the items prepared for them and disappeared as fast as they had appeared.

Dzunia and her mother were happy and proud not only to undertake such a big responsibility, but also to be able to take part in the struggle to liberate Poland. They never even mentioned the danger resulting from their involvement in the illegal organization.

Maria became a member of the AK underground group in Starachowice as well. She was there almost every week. Soon after arriving she reported for duty in her contact place. Very often, she was sent to the partisans in the forest with urgent messages.

Zdzislaw left his family and also joined the AK "forest boys" under the command of the famous "Ponury". His squad was in the neighboring woods. Zdzislaw's wife and their small daughter became completely dependent on Dziunia and her mother.

The patriotic atmosphere permeating the Slowik family's home had an influence on me. I also wanted to help fight the Germans and to make my personal contribution to their final defeat. Baking biscuits for the partisans, meeting the "forest boys" during the night, doing small errands for the AK gave me a sense of being part of an army fighting against my deadly enemy.

Warmer days arrived and Karola started to work on the small patches of garden assigned to her by Helena. She wanted to plant vegetables, recently scarce in the market. However, she did not believe that she would still be in Starachowice to harvest. She joked that she would give the fruit of her work as a goodbye gift to Helena.

The thought of leaving Starachowice evoked in Karola nostalgia for the life she had had before the war which had been brutally terminated by the Germans. She talked very often about the years she had spent in Lodz, about her friends and her social activities. Dziunia also missed her pre-war way of living. She wanted to return to her job in the post office as soon as possible, and again be with the people with whom she had worked for many years. Both women dreamed aloud about an independent Poland, freed from German occupation. They wanted the same Poland they had had before the war.

I could not even dream about my future. After the

cataclysm which had destroyed my world and killed my people, I was unable to visualize my life after the war. But at the same time, I was certain that I did not want to live in the Poland I remembered from before the war. I differed on this subject from Dziunia, her mother and all the people whom I had met in the Slowik home.

Anti-Semitism was the cause of my deep aversion to pre-war Poland. There was one national secondary school (3) in the City of Konskie for the whole district and for the neighboring cities of Opoczno and Skarzysko. *"Numerus clausus"* was the rule for accepting Jewish children into the national high schools. Only two to three percent of the total students admitted could be Jewish. I was one of the lucky ones who had the chance to study in the high school in Konskie until the outbreak of the war. During the three years I attended school there, I was humiliated by students and discriminated against by teachers many times.

I well remembered an episode that had occurred in the last year of my studies. There were two Jewish girls among 50 students in my French class. On this memorable day, the other Jewish girl was absent. When all the students gathered in the classroom, one boy, Adam Klusek, took the stand and demanded that I leave the room. He wanted, as he loudly explained, to call a meeting "in a pure Polish atmosphere", without Jews being present. As a result, I was forced to leave the classroom. My departure was followed by general applause, laughter and anti-Semitic epithets. I had to wait in the corridor, behind the closed door of my classroom, until the arrival of the teacher. After he had learned what had happened, he did not come to my defense. I was a good student and had helped many Polish students in mathematics and physics. However, during this episode nobody objected to the insulting way I was treated and later nobody had to account for the conduct.

All the students addressed each other by their first names,

but I was called only by my last name. By ignoring my first name, they probably wanted to demonstrate that a Jewish girl was different and not as good as a Polish one.

There were two students to a bench in the classrooms. Never did a Polish student share the bench with me. When there was an uneven number of Jewish and Christian students, two single places were left unoccupied. Polish students would rather sit alone than share the same bench with a Jew. No one in my class had social contact with me either in school or at home.

I did not attend school during such important Jewish holidays as Rosh Hashanah and Yom Kippur. Some teachers introduced difficult new material on these days and assigned homework. They would test Jewish students on this material and check their homework the first day after the holidays. Thus, I had to find out what new topic had been taught during my absence. There were only two girls among fifty students in the class who were willing to share this material with me. Krystyna Wielgosinska, the best student of the class, was one of them. Usually, in the evening after our holiday, I knocked at her door. She would meet me with her notes in the dark corridor. She would show me the material covered and the assigned lessons. However, she never invited me into her home and never introduced me to her family. Lodzia Czarnocka was the other student to whom I could turn with these kinds of questions. She was the daughter of Count Tarnowski's employee. Lodzia used to give me all the information in the courtyard, always in a hurry and always wanting me to leave as soon as possible. She never invited me into her home or introduced me to her family either.

My brother, who had finished high school in Konskie, couldn't enter medical school in Warsaw for two consecutive years because of the rule of "*numerus nulus*" for Jews in some departments of Polish universities.

The thought of living in this kind of country, where I had

been humiliated and had no right to study, was not appealing to me. I was able to dream about the end of the war, but I couldn't think about the time after that.

One night I noticed the door between the kitchen where I slept and Dziunia and her mother's bedroom was open during the night. Dziunia always closed it before going to bed. At first I thought that the door had not been properly closed and had opened by itself. During the following nights the door remained open. I understood the meaning of this simple gesture. Dziunia and Karolina Slowik were letting me know, in a tactful and gentle way, that they had really accepted me in their home. My feelings of gratitude were enormous. It was the end of the spring of 1943.

---

(1) GL (Gwardia Ludowa – People's Guard) created by the Party of Polish Workers in June, 1942 was an underground, fighting organization.
(2) AK (Armia Krajowa – National Army) was the underground, military organization under the authority of the Polish Government in exile in London.
(3) The national high school was owned and governed by the State of Poland.

During the warm days of the spring and summer of 1943, I often had to leave the safety of our home and spend time outside its protective walls. It was customary that the intensive housework had to be done in the open air whenever weather permitted. It was much easier to do it this way. For example, washing in the courtyard excluded carrying water and wood up and down the stairs. Drying the wash on the lines behind the house eliminated walking up on a ladder to the attic with a heavy load of wet linen. Sunny days were also conducive to airing the bedding, cleaning the carpets and to other similar tasks. In addition to the housework, I also spent a lot of time in the courtyard caring for the angora rabbits given to Dziunia by someone whom she had helped. The rabbits, well-fed, regularly cleaned, and kept in the open air grew and multiplied very fast. We bred them as a source of food should the war cut us off from any other supply. I planned to use their beautiful hair for knitting sweaters for Dziunia and Karola.

Now that I was doing work in the courtyard, I had to spend more time with the tenants of our house. I tried to be especially nice and helpful to them. I tried to project an image of myself as a pleasant and happy girl. I wanted to be liked by the neighbors. I believed that their positive opinion of me would protect me from suspicions of being Jewish.

There were five apartments in our house, two on the second and three on the ground floor. All of them consisted of one room and a kitchen. Our apartment number five and Helena's number four were upstairs. Apartment two and three opened to the courtyard and one was at the front. Family Praga, a young couple with a baby boy and their cousin Wanda lived in number two. Wanda, who recently came from the country, took care of the baby and helped with the housework. She was a plain peasant girl. Her movements were apathetic and clumsy. She always gave the impression of being scared, unhappy and lost. Most of the time, she didn't understand what was wanted of her. The difficulties she faced overwhelmed her. She angrily grumbled about her family's incomprehensible demands and groundless complaints. Early every morning, regardless of the weather, I heard her heavy footsteps. She was on her way to church. Wanda was my age. In spite of our differences, she appealed to me. I saw the symbol and the core of Polish ethnicity in her. She was the model of an average peasant Polish girl and I often tried to imitate her characteristic ways and sayings. I wanted to call on all the saints for help with the same ease; to make the sign of the cross on everything I touched; to be so clear as to what should and should not be said and thought. Nobody could suspect Wanda of being a Jewess and even such a thought was funny to me.

I had the impression that she was interested in me as well, mostly because I was "the girl from Warsaw". She showed me a certain respect, but in some situations she was truly amused by my clumsiness. She labeled any incompetence in me "Jewish". When I wrung the wet linen in a different direction than she did, unsuccessfully tried to catch a chicken, or held a struggling rabbit, she laughed, telling me I was doing things "the Jewish way". Although in her primitive language "the Jewish way" meant "different", the sound of this expression always caused a particular anxiety in me.

Mrs. Praga, Wanda's boss and cousin, was a blonde with a snub nose. She liked gossip and enjoyed spreading it in an exaggerated version. Always curious about what was going on in the neighborhood, she was the first to hear about it. Her language retained a peasant dialect in spite of having lived in the city for many years. Often I heard her loud, piercing voice when she shouted and cursed Wanda. Mr. Praga earned a living by buying food in the neighboring villages and selling it for a profit in Starachowice. He also traded unpurified alcohol called "bimber", which was produced in the country. Often the drunken Pragas' stormy arguments disturbed the silence in our house. This family expressed their vivid hatred toward Jews at every possible occasion. Their anti-Semitism, alcoholism and violent characteristics kept me on guard in their presence.

Apartment number three was occupied by an older couple with a teenage boy. The man of the house had held a high position before the war. The neighbors remembered that and treated him with respect, although they considered the couple to be strange and antisocial. At present, nobody in this family earned a living, and their financial difficulties were well known.

A couple with a daughter of my sister's age lived in apartment number one. The sight of this girl, who looked so like Helenka, made my yearning for her more intense. I thought about the different paths the lives of these two small girls had taken. My neighbor's child had a perfect chance to survive the war, while Helenka's life trembled in the balance. The Polish girl could play carefree surrounded by friendly people, while the Jewish girl was without basic childhood privileges and grew up in an atmosphere of constant fear.

The father of the girl was employed in the munitions factory in Starachowice. Early in the morning, he would leave for work and late in the evening, he would return home. Twice a day at the same time to the minute, I heard his footsteps in the garden. The sounds of his arrival and departure served me as a clock. Sofia, his wife, a pretty woman, worked at home as a dressmaker. During the warm days, the clatter of her sewing machine out on the front porch could be heard in the house. Sofia was a close friend of Mrs. Praga and the two women spent a lot of time together constantly whispering secrets.

All the inhabitants of our building treated Karola Slowik with great respect, and considered her a real "grande dame". Nobody would dare to say a vulgar word or behave improperly in her presence. On the other hand, Dziunia was a person whom they adored and felt very friendly toward. They often asked her for help and she was always willing to oblige. They considered her to have been sent by Providence to make wartime less difficult.

There were long talks and hot discussions during the warm days in our courtyard. Sometimes the neighbors talked about their personal problems, even about the closest members of their families. They openly expressed political views, comments about the activities of the underground organizations and about the future of Poland. It was obvious, based on the honesty with which they shared their opinions, that nobody feared being denounced to the Germans by the other tenants of our building.

Very often, the neighbors gathered in the courtyard and conversed about the Jews. All of them had something very negative to say about them. Jews were swindlers, the cause of the pre-war poverty, masters of international intrigues, carriers of diseases, personifications of the devil and so on. They talked about massive murders of the Jews with such indifference - as if the Jews were animals, not humans. I never heard a word of sympathy concerning the Jews' present fate.

I tried to avoid the social gatherings in the courtyard. However, I did not want to be suspected of separating myself from the neighbors. Therefore, I sometimes had to join their circle. I always expected that sooner or later they would start to talk about Jews and I waited for that moment with growing fear. I knew that when I would hear the word "Jew", a wave of heat would go through my body and red spots would appear on my face. Although I tried with all my willpower to prevent or stop this reaction, I was less and less successful at it.

Sometimes I was able to leave the gathering at just the right moment and would wait until I recovered. Sometimes I tried to divert their attention from my strange warming to something else. I pretended that I dropped an object on the ground, was struck by pain or choked from a sudden cough. The attack of heat usually lasted no more than a few minutes and it would make me resistant to the word "Jew" for some time. When the redness had disappeared from my face, I was able to rejoin the group, and to keep myself calm and indifferent even to the most anti-Semitic remarks.

I had the strange impression that my personality was composed of two hostile human beings and each one waned to destroy the other. The one-me did everything to hide the life-threatening secret; and the second-me wanted the secret to be publicly disclosed. Constantly reinventing new ways of hiding my violent blushing was my only protection from the destructive second-me.

The neighbors were interested in my life in Warsaw. They asked about my school, family and friends. They wanted to know my father's profession, what my mother was doing, how many siblings I had. They wondered why my family did not visit me and when I would return to Warsaw. They joked about me always staying at home and not looking for some young man's companionship. In the fairy tale I invented for them, my father had been a professional officer in the Polish army and had never returned home after being called up in 1939. My mother had a weak heart and very often suffered from this illness. My only brother supported our mother and took care of her.

Describing my fictional family, I tried to use real elements of my past life. I really did have one brother (1) and my late mother had heart disease. However, I decided to change my father's occupation. I thought a Polish army officer would appeal more to these people than a dentist.

The neighbors' inquiring questions always prompted fear in me. I did not know if they were simply curious or dangerously suspicious. I talked about that with Dziunia and we both agreed we needed more confirmation of my false biography. We knew that letters from Warsaw would do the trick. The appearance of a postman with an envelope addressed to me would be immediately noticed and commented on. However, Dziunia couldn't find anybody trustworthy enough to implement this plan.

We decided to stage my mother's visit. During one gathering of the neighbors, I told them about it. I played the role of an excited and happy daughter who could not wait to see her mother. When the date of my mother's "arrival" was near, I started elaborate preparation. The aroma of baking and cooking filled the whole building. I borrowed a folding bed from a neighbor, covered with fresh linen and put it in the kitchen. Helena was a major witness to the entire preparation and told everyone about it . Thanks to her, the tenants knew exactly when and how Maryla's mother, Mrs. Czajkowska, would arrive.

On the day of supposed arrival Karola, Dziunia, Stasia and even little Alinka (Zdzislaw's wife and daughter) went with me to the train station. The train from Warsaw came in on time. I ran along the platform looking for my mother among the many passengers who had arrived in Starachowice. I checked the empty compartments and even asked the conductor about an elderly lady who had boarded the train at the Central Station in Warsaw. I pretended to be disappointed and upset when I learned that my mother had not arrived. My performance was good because Stasia, who did not know the truth, consoled me the whole time. I continued to play the role of the worried daughter until one day I told the neighbors about my mother's health problems, which had forced her to postpone the visit. It seemed that everyone believed my story.

Later, when the questions started to intensify again, I made a new plan to improve my credibility in the Polish world. This time, I decided to find a young man and start going out with him.

Stasia Cadrzynska was the closest of Dziunia's friends. They worked together in the same factory store. Stasia lived with her older brother Karol. I had met him when they visited us at Christmastime. They had lived in the City of Katowice (2) before, where Karol had a high position in coal mining as an engineer. At the beginning of the war, he lost his job and they were expelled by the Germans from the city. They settled in Starachowice. Karol did not want to work for the Germans any more and stayed at home. Stasia complained that her brother felt very lonely in a city where he had no friends. Because Karol seemed to be the right person for the main character in my new plan, Dziunia arranged a meeting.

Karol invited me for a walk one sunny Sunday. After that day, we spent an afternoon together once a week. Karol was forty years old. He appeared to be nice, warm-hearted and gentle. He told me about the sudden death of his parents when he was very young. This tragedy made him the sole protector of his younger sister. His story was moving.

The general opinion about Karol was very positive. In spite of our short acquaintance and the big difference in age, the neighbors soon designated him as my fiancé. They greeted us with approval when we walked together through the courtyard. My plan produced the desired results and was also pleasant for me. As time passed, Karol lost his uneasiness and reserve in my presence. He talked more freely about his feelings, thoughts and plans. I was getting used to this gentle, good person. I started to think that such a decent fellow would accept the truth about me without a problem.

One Sunday we went for a long walk and reached the top of a hill from where a beautiful view of Starachowice could be seen. We rested there. Karol showed me different parts of the city and the huge space occupied by the munitions factory. Suddenly he changed the subject. He became very emotional. He told me with real anger about his hatred of the Germans for their brutal devastation of his beloved country, for ruining his private life and his professional career. He hated the Germans for everything. However, he felt a real gratitude toward them for cleansing Poland of Jews.

"Not long ago, the Germans murdered hundreds of Jews on this hill," he said to me. "We Poles should build Hitler a monument here for solving the Jewish problem for us. Thanks to him, a free Poland is going always be without Jews." The usually gentle face of a warm-hearted person was now full of hatred. It was a hatred of my people.

Luckily, this time I did not have any visible reaction to his anti-Semitic words. I did not feel any heat inside me, no muscle on my face moved and it retained its normal color. Listening to him, I remained calm, as if I shared his feelings completely. I saw that Karol did not expect a different reaction from me.

A few times I had heard this comment about the monument to Hitler as thanks for liquidating the Jews. I heard it the first time on the train from Skarzysko to Warsaw, then my neighbors in our courtyard repeated it and now Karol Cadrzynski said the same thing. I realized that this expression of enormous hatred toward the Jews, showing a complete lack of basic human feelings for the whole Jewish nation, represented the general Polish opinion. These feelings of hatred were shared by common peasant women, average city people and also by the educated person. I understood how isolated and small the group of decent human beings like Dzunia, her mother, sister and Stanislaw was in the huge sea of people with murderous feelings toward the Jews.

I met Karol only a few more times. When he proposed a more serious relationship, I refused, giving my young age as an excuse. Karol stopped coming to us.

One night I looked through the window at the terrain where the Jewish camp had been. There was darkness where before reflectors had lighted the surrounding fences every few minutes. It made me angry with myself that I hadn't noticed when the liquidation of the camp had occurred. I felt as if I had lost a close friend and forgotten about her funeral. I had a terrifying thought of remaining the only Jewish person in the Jew-hating Polish world.

I recalled the satiric poem I had read before the war about

the editor of the Warsaw Newspaper, Adolf Nowaczynski. He was a well-known writer, notorious for his hatred of Jews. In this satire Mr. Adolf, after a whole day of writing an article for the Sunday edition, full of anti-Semitic slogans, fell asleep. In his dream he saw Poland without Jews. They all had magically disappeared from his country. "Polishness" was everywhere as he had always wanted it to be. The Poles were going to Poles for Polish things. The traditional Jewish attire vanished from the streets. Jewish newspapers were no longer printed. The Poles were purchasing, selling and bargaining in the Jewish district of Warsaw.

Mr. Adolf, still in his dream, started to write an article for the following Sunday. But this time his task became unusually difficult. His anger toward Jews and the Jewish "chutzpah" spurred him on. He wanted to encourage the Poles to keep fighting the Jews, to protect the universities from them, to take commerce into their own hands. But there were no longer any Jews in Poland and there was no one to fight. With the disappearance of Jews he had lost his purpose in writing.

The satire ended with Adolf Nowaczynski's dream-wish. He wanted to look for a Jewish child all over Poland. He hoped he could find it, lost in some remote part of the country. He would be happy to take this last Jewish soul to his home and bring it up. This way he would have consolation in his old age.

I could not free myself from a persistent thought. The apocalyptic prediction of the Jews' extermination, as described in the poem, had come true. Was it I who was destined for the role of a "last Jewish soul"?

---

(1) My brother Jerzy Rudny was born in 1919 as Jerzy Kon in Konskie. He escaped from Konskie to the Soviet Union in 1940, where he survived the war. At the present time, he lives in Sweden.
(2) The City of Katowice was in the part of Poland annexed to the Reich during the WWII..

WITH THE PARTISANS

The AK (Home Army) in Starachowice planned an attack on the money-collector. Dziunia, who knew the collector's schedule, took part in the preparations for this raid. The armed partisans were to take all the money from him which he transported from the stores to the German headquarters on the side street of Starachowice.

Almost all the members of the Slowik family were now actively involved in the AK conspiracy work. There was a liaison point called "the mailbox" in our home. Zdzislaw belonged to the partisans and Maria was a liaison officer between the city and forest groups. Often some high-ranking officers of the AK visited our home. They would come with instructions for Dziunia or Maria or just to collect material sent to "the mailbox". I had been introduced to them and they knew me as a close relative of the Slowiks. Although I did not formally belong to the organization, the AK authorities asked me for help in the attack on the money-collector.

I had contradictory feelings about my participation in this action. On the one hand, I knew that my involvement could create more danger for me than for the average Polish person. It would require me to spend some time on the streets, mingling with the crowds. However, since the episode with the boy who had recognized me as a Jewess in the marketplace, I avoided being alone in the streets of the city. On the other had, I was thrilled by the possibility of taking part in an action against the Germans.

Finally, Dziunia and Karola made the decision for me. Although they comprehended the danger, they wanted me to collaborate with the AK. There could be no explanation of why a young member of their family such as I would refuse the request of the underground organization. They thought that such an attitude could arouse unnecessary suspicions.

A few days before the action, I went to the factory store at the time the collector was there and I familiarized myself with his face and personality. Next, I went to the specified place at the precise time where, in turn, I was looked at by the unknown conspirators. However, I was never able to identify the people observing me.

The day of the action was warm and sunny. At the designated hour, I was waiting on the bridge over a small brook, as if I were resting after a walk. Very few passers-by were on the street. Not far from me, two men holding bicycles were talking loudly. I suspected them to be partisans but, of course, I wasn't certain of that. When the collector on his bike reached the bridge, I took my scarf off my head and combed my hair. I identified the person for whom the partisans were waiting with this agreed-upon signal. This was my sole part in the action. I returned home with a very pleasant feeling of having taken part in the general fight against the Germans.

Soon after, we were notified that the partisans had been caught in this action and imprisoned by the Gestapo. Nobody knew if the seizure of the partisans was accidental or the result of treason in the ranks of the organization. It was probable that the imprisoned men would betray the co-conspirators under torture. Because they had known me they could also describe my role in the attack.

Irena, a high-ranking officer of the AK in Starachowice, recommended far-reaching precautions for the near future. She closed "the mailbox" in our home and took away all the illegal materials we had stored in the attic. She advised me to leave Starachowice for the time being. She suggested I join the neighboring partisan unit and await the clarification of this situation over there.

Karola was against this idea. She thought my life with the partisans would be more dangerous than at home. Dziunia, on the contrary, considered my leaving home a good solution to many problems. I personally was drawn to the life in the military battalion far away from the reach of the Germans. I was convinced that the AK's recommendation would free me from any suspicion of being Jewish. In addition, my absence from home could be used to reinforce the stories I had told about my life. The neighbors would know that I went to see my mother in Warsaw who had fallen ill. However, I did not volunteer my opinion and left the decision to Dziunia and Karola. Finally, both women agreed that I should leave home and stay with the partisans for now.

I said goodbye to Dziunia and her mother early in the morning. I found that it was difficult to leave behind these two women who had become very dear to me. Maria, who had arrived from Konskie the day before, guided me to the partisans' squad. At first, we walked along the sandy road among the trees. We collected mushrooms in baskets which were to be an explanation for our presence in the wilderness should the Germans suddenly appear. Then we left the road and entered the thick forest. There were no paths. Maria knew the right direction, guided by the invisible signs. Suddenly, two armed men in civilian clothes stopped us. They asked us for the password and when they received it, they gave us further directions. We reached the small clearing after a whole day's march. The view was extraordinary there. The young men were sitting on the grass beneath a white/red Polish flag fluttering in the air. I was moved. I had come across the free Poland.

The commander of the partisans squad, pseudonym "Grot", was thirty years old and looked like a military man. His unit of forty or so people was part of the AK underground army under the command of the notorious "Ponury" (Gloomy).

"Grot" greeted us warmly. He already knew the history of the unsuccessful attack on the money-collector in Starachowice and was expecting my arrival. We were invited to supper after a short rest. A few officers, including Zdzislaw Slowik, were with us at the table in the middle of the clearing. Maria, who was well known here from her previous visits, was greeted by everyone.

No real names were used for the sake of the partisans' families living under the Germans. Therefore, I had to choose some pseudonym for myself. When somebody suggested "Raspberry" for my new "forest" name, I agreed without hesitation.

A merry atmosphere permeated the table. There was a lot of food, and even more "bimber", the unpurified alcohol produced from potatoes by peasants from the neighborhood. During the general conversations, I learned about an event that had happened a few days before. The partisan reconnaissance found a lone Jew hiding behind the trees. The commander ordered the Jew to be shot. When I bravely asked "why", I was told that this was a safer way for everyone. I thought with irony that they were right to some extent. Nothing could endanger the dead Jew anymore.

"Grot" directed me to a tent in the middle of the camp. There was a soldier put on guard in front of it all night long. After Maria returned home the next day, I was the only woman in the squad.

I was assigned to the sanitary service. At this time there were neither sick nor wounded soldiers in the camp, but that could change rapidly after the first action. Kazik, the young doctor from Skarzysko, told me that he could provide only very poor medical help. He lacked the necessary surgical instruments, bandages and medications. He used the unpurified alcohol to disinfect and anesthetize. Zdzislaw shared with me a secret about Kazik's wife who was a Jewess baptized some time ago. Someone notified the Germans about that. Kazik was lucky to escape into the forest, but his wife's fate was unknown and he feared the worst.

"Grot's" military camp was then situated at the side of a small brook. However, a plan to move it to a new location was in preparation. The extended camping in one place was dangerous for such a big group of people. The Germans could have enough time to trace the squad in the forest. The whole of "Grot's" unit was divided into small groups with a commander for each one. The groups were assigned daily to the different tasks inside and outside the camp. The partisans were young boys mostly from small villages. They had been introduced to a harsh and dangerous military life. There were not sufficient guns for all the soldiers in the camp and they were eager to capture the needed arms from the Germans. Weapons were assigned only to those soldiers who were going into action. Our unit was considered to be a cavalry unit because we kept horses in the camp. Thanks to them, the partisans could reach distant places in a relatively short time. The "forest-boys" spent a lot of time caring for these animals and they did it with visible pleasure.

Getting food for such a big group of young men was a very serious problem. The partisans, who were assigned the task of acquiring provisions, could not always supply the camp with an adequate amount and variety of food. There were days when we would eat only one thing such as eggs, bacon or barley. There were also times when the unit sent for food would return without it. Then all of us in the camp were starving. However, we almost always had "bimber" and that kept the boys warm and in good spirits. In the evenings we gathered around the hot coals of the campfire and we sang folk and patriotic songs. The singing voices probably could be heard far away, but nobody seemed to care. The most beautiful ballads were about the heroism of "Ponury", their undefeated chief commander. The partisans adored him and were ready to sacrifice their young lives for their great leader.

I was trained in firing the rifle. The disassembling and then putting together different kinds of guns and rifles was quite an easy task for me, but I had difficulties with target-shooting. I didn't know why, but I was unable to close one eye only. I always had to open or close both eyes simultaneously to the joy of the watching boys. Just to aim sharply, I had to cover one eye with my hand. This disability would be dangerous during a confrontation with the enemy. I only had a few lessons in shooting because there was a lack of ammunition, making each bullet precious.

"Grot" gave me a small pistol, a so-called number four, and the right bullets for it as a gift. Possession of the gun gave me a pleasant feeling of safety. I promised myself that I would use it against myself if the situation called for it.

Horse riding also was difficult for me. After a few rides, I overcame my fear of big animals. I even felt some personal connection with my horse. I learned how to harness, fast-mount and dismount him. But I couldn't coordinate the movement of my body with the rhythm of his gallop nor hold him strongly with my legs. Although I was supposed to sit straight in the saddle, I felt more secure leaning forward holding the horse's neck.

After a few days in the forest, and a short course in target shooting and horse riding, I was assigned to the first action outside the camp. We left the camp late in the afternoon and rode a long time in the roadless woods. I was in the middle of the column of about ten partisans as ordered by the commander. It was dark when we stopped at the edge of the forest. We waited under the trees for the return of the reconnaissance squad. When we learned the Germans were not in the immediate neighborhood, we galloped to the nearby settlement.

We reached the big farm in the middle of the village. The commander put soldiers on guard in front of different buildings. My assignment was to watch the main house and not let anybody in or out. I held the gun in my hands ready to shoot. I was moved by my responsibility. I felt a strong bond with the co-partisans. I was aware of the danger. I was not afraid. The feeling of sharing a common fate with the others was calming.

There was silence.

After some time, the commander left the house together with a farmer dressed only in a long nightshirt and drawers. Now I was ordered to watch over the people inside the building. There was a lamenting woman with several crying children. I stood in the door pointing the gun at them.

We returned to the camp at full gallop. I concentrated my whole attention on the horse, holding his neck with all my strength. The horse galloped between the trees. I lost my orientation and the contact with the boys from the unit who were scattered in the forest. Luckily, the horse found his way to the camp and I saw the familiar place among the trees by dawn. I felt as if I had returned to my real home. Our action was successful. We brought a lot of food with us.

Weeks passed. The nights became cold and it was often raining. My clothes were always wet and I was unable to dry them. Lice were in everything I wore and I had to spend all my free time hunting them. I was hungry when there was no food in the camp and I drank stinking "bimber" when I was shaking from the cold.

A few times, I took part in the actions. Sometimes they were far away from camp. I could not learn to ride the galloping horse with my back straight or shoot with one eye closed. But I could sleep during the long nightly marches walking in a row with the partisans. I did not know the names of the places where we were sent or the people whom we came to see during the night. I knew most of them willingly collaborated with the partisans. At times, there were some individuals who were spying for the Germans and our sudden appearance in the darkness of the night was for them a threat or even a punishment.

Though I was under constant danger in the camp and during the actions, I felt safer in the forest than in Starachowice. The small gun I always kept with me helped me feel this way.

In the forest, I did not react with blushing to the word "Jew". I did not experience waves of heat in my body when the partisans made jokes about the Jews in my presence.

One Sunday, Maria appeared in the camp. She brought information from the AK authorities. The Germans had arrested no one else in connection with the attack on the money-collector during the time of my absence from Starachowice. The AK assumed the imprisoned partisans had not denounced the members of the underground organization. My homecoming was considered safe. Dziunia and Karola were missing me. I said goodbye to "Grot" and his partisans and I returned my small pistol with regret.

DZIUNA

Maria guided me through the forest. After many hours of walking we reached the suburbs of Starachowice. It was evening when we arrived at Stasia's, Zdzislaw Slowik's wife. Karola and Dziunia waited for us there. All three women greeted me very affectionately, as if I were a dear member of the family who was returning home after a long separation. They were clearly upset by my emaciated face and worn-out clothes.

Karola regretted that she had succumbed to pressure from the underground organization and had agreed, too hastily, to my escape into the forest. She blamed herself for the harsh life I had while being with the partisans. At one moment, she approached me and said, "I will never allow anybody or anything to separate us again. We are together now united by a common fate. What happens to you also happens to us."

Her emotional words moved me to the core and were the highest reward for all the difficult times I had had at their home. I knew well that it was I who had been the cause of her worries, anger and crying during the first few months of my presence. Almost every evening, she demanded that Dziunia threw me out from her house. Her pleading, "I don't want her in my home. Tell her to leave", still had a fearful echo in my memory. I saw now the extreme change of her attitude toward me.

Dziunia greeted me with a spontaneous delight characteristic of her. Right away, she told me all the happenings during my absence, repeating constantly how much she had missed me. Even Stasia, who mostly was interested in her husband's well-being, openly showed me how pleased she was that I had returned home.

Dziunia and her mother loved Zdzislaw's wife. They trusted her and valued her practical wisdom. Stasia knew about the family's involvement in the underground organization and

161

about the existence of the liaison-point in our home. She also was aware of my participation in the attack on the money-collector and about the consequences that forced me to find refuge in the forest. She knew about Dziunia's manipulation of ration coupons in the factory store.

It seemed to me that Stasia had been trusted with all the family secrets except for one. My true identity was hidden from her. She and her husband were not told that I was a Jewess. I suspected that the reason for this secrecy was not Dziunia's or Karola's lack of trust, but rather fear that their son and daughter-in-law would not approve of risking their own lives in order to save a Jewish one.

After a short rest, I improved my general appearance to a decent state and we all went home together at the time which coincided with the arrival of the train from Warsaw. Helena and the other neighbors greeted me in a friendly manner. Their questions about life in the Polish Capital and my mother's health were the obvious indication that they believed in my trip home to Warsaw.

One year had passed since I appeared in the middle of the night in the apartment of the Slowik women. I clearly remembered the impression their clean, bright and warm room made on me. It gave me the feeling that this was the safest place on earth, as if it were far beyond German reach. These two Polish women in this quiet place were like a magical realization of the dreams I had during the long weeks of my homelessness among strangers. I had reached the limit of my endurance then. I did not have any more strength left I in me. Each cell of my body was immensely tired. I had to forget about the constant German pursuit. I had to close my eyes and fall asleep.

I noticed then that my looks and sudden appearance scared both women. I saw their horrified eye-contacts. I felt their anxiety and ill-will toward me. I was aware that I had intruded on their life. I knew I was not welcome there. But I also knew that regardless of all their reluctance, I must stay there. I was unable to leave this place. It was my only refuge. A small corner in these women's home was literally a matter of my life or death. My instinct for self-preservation forced me to hold on to what I had just found with all my strength. I felt that I must be blind and deaf to everything which prevented me from staying there. I was determined not to leave their apartment of my own free will and not to allow anybody to throw me out.

The anniversary of my arrival probably evoked some reminiscences in Dziunia also. One evening, when we were alone in the kitchen, she started to talk about her feelings during that memorable night.

She already understood who the alleged Maria from Warsaw was when I stood outside the closed door. My sudden appearance took her by surprise. The possible deadly consequences of this encounter terrified her. She was aware of Helena's watchful eyes and suspicious mind. She knew how frightened her mother would become and she tried to protect her hiding her own fear. When she had closed the door and looked at me for the first time in the lit room, her horror intensified. She saw on my face and in my manners a repulsive aggressiveness bordering on open hostility. She had a feeling that I would present a physical danger to her. A Jewess stood in her room and this fact was punishable by the death of the whole family. Furthermore, this Jewish girl, bearing such a danger, had an evil looking face.

Unable to throw me out, she did not know how to react. She was afraid of the Germans, of Helena, of me, and of the whole situation I had put her in. She tried to hide her own helplessness from her mother. She couldn't stand my presence in her room any longer and just told me to go to the kitchen. Later, under the cover of darkness, she tried to overcome her nervousness by convincing herself I would stay with them only one night. The next day Mrs. Petronela Rudna, my relative, who had arrived in Starachowice several weeks ago, would

163

take me to her place.

Dziunia's recollections were shocking to me. I now learned how clearly she had read in my face everything I had tried to conceal. I confessed to her how correctly she had estimated my state of desperation at the time. The fact that I was sincerely able to tell her about that let me realize the magnitude of the changes which had occurred in our relationship. After one year, I not only lived with these Slowik women met accidentally, but we had become emotionally attached to each other.

During these past months, I had gotten to know something about Karola's and Dziunia's past. At a very young age Dziunia had lost her father, who had been the sole family provider. Her thirty-something year old widowed mother was completely unprepared for an independent life. At the age of eighteen she had married a much older man. Her husband always treated her as if she were a child. After his death, Karola Slowik was left without any means of supporting herself and her three children. Dziunia, the oldest of the children, was forced to become the caretaker for her mother, Maria, the two-year-younger sister and Zdzislaw, the five-year-younger brother. Her job, as a telephone operator in the state owned Main Post Office in the City of Lodz, provided a small but steady income and financial security for the whole Slowik family.

After a few years, Karola remarried. The second husband was a handsome young man with whom she fell in love. Unluckily, this new marriage did not last long. Karola took her husband's departure and the ultimate finality of her short marriage very badly. Her personal tragedy and the protracted divorce process caused her extreme suffering.

Dziunia never mentioned the time of her mother's second marriage. I even noticed that whenever her mother started to talk about her divorced husband, Dziunia switched the subject of the conversation. It seemed to me that Karola blamed

Dziunia for her unsuccessful marriage. From loose fragments of information, I could picture what had happened. I suspected that Karola's husband and his young stepdaughter had fallen in love. Their mutual feeling brought about the family's tragedy.

That could explain why Dziunia, a very open person, never said anything about her emotional past. It would also clarify why she, an attractive, warm-hearted woman, has kept herself away from any serious relationship with a man. Karola's often-repeated statement that Dziunia would always remain with her to make up for youthful mistakes seemed to confirm my suspicions.

Karola's financial situation improved during the years preceding the outbreak of the war. She obtained a government license for the sale of cigarettes and alcohol. Maria married young and moved out. Zdzislaw enrolled in the military school away from the City of Lodz. Only Dziunia, the oldest daughter, remained with her mother.

Dziunia was seventeen years older than I, but she made an impression of being the same age. When she returned after a whole day's work in the factory store, she enlivened all of us. The very characteristic sound of her voice and her quick flow of words immediately filled the apartment. She was eager to share with us everything that had occupied her mind during the day. Thanks to her precise and picturesque descriptions, I could easily imagine the clients who had appeared in front of her wicket and the situations she had encountered.

Dziunia was an optimist and this attitude was the source of the power in her life. In addition, she had the ability to convey her conviction of a better tomorrow to others. She also had the gift of understanding the difficulties that others were going through. She felt their misery and suffering. These unusual elements of her character were somehow visible on her face, attracting people who clung to her. Often a stranger, a first-time client, who came only to collect the rations, could spend additional time just to tell Dziunia about his complicated problems, anticipating her understanding and advice. Repeatedly, Dziunia would learn later that her words had given needed hope and strength in the difficult moments of someone else's life.

This was why Dziunia was able to accept my presence in her home and tolerate the constant danger related to it. This was why she helped people by giving illegal rations of food, regardless of her personal risk. Her family, the neighbors, the members of different underground organizations and even strangers who asked for help, belonged to the long list of people under her care. She, herself, was reluctant to say a word about her generosity and always minimized her role, calling it an "insignificant friendly favor". Sometimes, by accident, we were able to see how much people valued Dziunia.

One day a strange girl came with two fresh eggs for Miss Dziunia. Such a gift was expensive during the winter and the donor did not look as if she could afford it. It appeared that she had worked in the munitions factory, but had lost her job one year before. Because she had been the sole breadwinner for her old parents and teenage brother, they all would have starved to death were it not, as she put it, "for Miss Dziunia's golden heart".

I was full of admiration for Dziunia's quiet, unpretentious courage in many dangerous situations. Under everyday conditions easily excited, she knew how to exercise emotional restraint when it was necessary. Her behavior seemed to belittle the threat and had a quieting effect on everyone around her. I suspected that Dziunia paid with her health for her calm during numerous German checks in the factory store. The stomach pain she often suffered could have been caused by suppressed nervousness.

Dzunia was a great patriot and she loved Poland with all her heart. The quickest defeat of the Germans and the liberation of her homeland was the most important thing to her. She was personally connected with the AK (Home Army), the ranks of which also included Maria and Zdzislaw. However, she supported each group fighting against the Germans, even those with an extreme political agenda. Stanislaw introduced her to the leftist underground organization GL (People's Army). She remained in touch with this group and often provided help to its members. Dziunia also systematically gave food provisions to two brothers who were active fighters in the rightist and anti-Semitic underground organization NSZ (National Armed Forces). Irena, a high ranking officer of the AK in Starachowice, was an advocate for these two men.

Dziunia was a devoted Catholic, but at the same time, she was very tolerant of people who had a different approach to religion than she did. She respected Stanislaw who openly manifested an uncompromising atheism. Although we attended church services every Sunday together, she never tried to convince me about the existence of God or the superiority of Catholicism over other religions. She clearly considered my church attendance as a necessary cover-up and not as a way of converting me to Christianity. Karola, on the contrary, told me many times that my conversion to Catholicism had been her dream. Dziunia responded to her mother's remarks with an enigmatic smile.

Catholicism seemed to me a very pretty religion. It would be pleasant to be a part of this church. The affiliation to it created a strong bond with the whole Polish nation of thirty million people. Catholicism gave hope to the believers that God had listened, Christ had loved, the Holy Virgin had understood and would guard them if it was needed.

I was still looking for a sign of God's existence and was unable to find it. I couldn't evoke the necessity of praying and all my attempts were only the outcome of my despair. However, I liked to attend the services in the church. The organ music moved me to some unknown emotional state. The congregation of praying people and their choral singing gave

167

me an illusion of belonging to the people surrounding me. On my knees, I felt humble and grateful for the fate which saved me and I forgot the painful question of why my dear people perished.

Yet I would never convert to Catholicism. I was born Jewish and all my family, friends and the people with whom I had lived for eighteen years were Jewish. They died terrible deaths because they were Jews. This tragedy made me feel more bonded with them than ever in my life. I was unable to break this bond even if I would like to.

Winter 1943/44 was extremely difficult for me. Very cold weeks went on and on as if the winter would not end.

My laced shoes, made to order before the war by a shoemaker in Konskie, were worn out, giving me very little protection against the cold. There were holes in both of them and I had to conceal them with pieces of fabric colored with shoe paste. Through the paper-thin soles, I could feel every clod of frozen ground and every stone on the road. I wrapped my feet with layers of paper and rags before going outdoors but they were often painfully cold. Since my shoes were in very bad shape, I worried that one day they would completely fall apart. Then I would be literally left barefoot in the winter weather. I had exceptionally long feet and even if Dziunia or Karola had been willing to share their shoes, they would have been too small for me.

I did not have any hope for acquiring a new pair of shoes. There was never any footwear for distribution in the factory store where Dziunia worked. The price for shoes made of leather, whether new or used, which sometimes appeared on the market, were astronomical for me. Even shoes with wooden soles, made now by the new generation of Polish shoemakers, were too costly. I did not have any money and Dziunia's financial resources were not sufficient for such an expense.

By now, my winter coat, made in 1938 in Konskie, was shredded and torn in many places. I had worn it constantly in the Ghetto, sometimes not even taking it off at night. It also protected me on chilly and cold days all year around in Starachowice. In the wintertime I added the fur collar to my coat which I removed for the warmer season.

All the pieces of my shabby wardrobe, always worn and often washed, were also falling apart although I tried to mend them constantly. When I appeared in the Slowik house at the end of 1942 I had nothing but what I wore on my back. I was dressed in a double layer of warm underwear, a woolen dress, a dark blue sweater and a winter coat.

Maria, concerned about my lack of clothing, decided to go to the church organist in Czarniecka Gora, where I, Sara and Helenka had spent the first night after escaping from the Ghetto. We had left two suitcases there with our underwear and clothes when we took flight from our host and his murderous friends in the middle of the night. I was against Maria's plan of going there. I did not want to endanger her for a few pieces of my clothes. The organist tried to kill us Jews and I was afraid that he would also be able to harm an Aryan. In spite of my concern, Maria went on with her plan. She stopped in Czarniecka Gora on her way from Starachowice to Konskie and appeared in the organist's house unexpectedly. She pretended to be sent by the AK (Home Army) for the suitcases left on November 2, 1942 by Jewish women whom this Polish underground organization had helped to escape from the Konskie Ghetto.

The organist was very surprised and visibly frightened. He said he had wanted very much to help these Jewish women but that they had been suspicious and ungrateful. They left his home in the middle of the night without a word of thanks. He did not deny that the Jewesses left two suitcases. However, he claimed that there was a burglary in his home and the thieves stole all of his and the Jewish refugees' possessions. Nevertheless, Maria's threats forced him to return some pieces of clothing allegedly left by the thieves. Thanks to Maria's trip, I recovered a much needed change of underwear and additional dresses. Unluckily, there were no shoes and no coat in the package.

I waited impatiently for the arrival of warmer days. According to the popular belief, the spring of 1944 would bring the ultimate defeat of the Germans and the end of the war. Again the refrain, "only until spring", was commonly repeated, now for the fourth year. The coming spring was synonymous with freedom.

The news about the progress of the Allied Armies was very good. In the East, the Soviet Army was moving ahead in a big semicircle liberating Smolensk, Kijow, Nowogrod and reaching Romania at the south end. The Western Forces had landed in southern Italy. The defeated Italian Army declared war on the Germans, once their ally. The leaders of the world, Roosevelt, Churchill and Stalin, met in Teheran to create a united plan for Hitler's defeat.

The big German cities and their factories were now constantly bombed by the American and English air forces. In November I heard about the huge air raids on Berlin and later on Hamburg. Polish people had become very optimistic. I also wanted to be infused with his happy feeling. I tried to create the map of Europe in my imagination and mark all the liberated cities. I followed every victory of the Allied Army in my mind. Their victories gave me the strength to endure each day and provided the reason for waiting for tomorrow. The German defeats were of the same significance as air and food. I believed in the approaching final hour of Nazism, but it was more and more difficult for me to wait for it. I became increasingly impatient and nervous. The progress of the Allied Army was too slow. The liberated cities were too far from Starachowice. The approaching Soviet Army that could rescue me was still too distant.

While the defeat of the Germans seemed to be more certain and real, my hope of surviving the last moments of their power and witnessing the liberation became weaker. Every passing day I tortured myself with distracting thoughts. I convinced myself that fate had mocked me in my naïve belief about surviving the war. I did not analyze what I really understood by the term "fate". It could be a malicious God or some unidentified force guiding the world or a simple coincidence. Most important was my conviction that this "fate" allowed me to feel secure sometimes, only to later make me see more clearly that my true place was with the murdered Jews. I was convinced that regardless of what I was doing and how I tried to defend myself, I would die in the last phase of the war.

This masochistic thinking drained my strength. Often I had the impression I was going out of my mind. In my imagination every favorable political news report forecasted not only the approaching end of the war, but also my inevitable death in the final hour of German power.

I was unable to suppress the fear that grew in me. Sometimes, mostly during the night, it choked me and made my heart beat very fast. I felt a bitter taste in my mouth and I was nauseated. A wave of heat covered my whole body. I was afraid. I was afraid of suspicions, of being recognized, of suffering. I was afraid of death more and more with each passing day.

One day, an accident happened that made me aware of how easily my fear was manifested when I was taken by surprise. I had been knitting a woolen suit for Karola. The wool came from the angora rabbits which I had taken care of for a long time. At first the raw animal hair was converted into knitting yarn and then dyed blue and white. I made a pattern for a two-part blue costume, a slightly broad skirt with a long, buttoned-front jacket. The skirt, the collar, the lapels were to be adorned with white stylized flowers. I already had experience in knitting sweaters. I used to earn some money making them to order in the Konskie Ghetto – most of the time with old wool from undone sweaters. I learned then to work very fast, almost automatically.

Once, when I was completely engrossed in my knitting, Helena, unnoticed by me, watched me working. Suddenly her voice caught me unaware.

"I never saw a Polish girl knitting so fast. Only the Jewesses used to work this way," she said.   Immediately, a hot wave covered my body and my cheeks flushed.

Horrified by my visible reaction, I threw the ball of wool away from my knees. It rolled under the bed and I crawled after it. These acrobatics gave me some time to cool off. Luckily, Helena did not notice my suddenly reddening face.

Although the Germans had been systematically defeated on the distant fronts, their behavior in Starachowice did not indicate that they would leave the city soon. They became even more brutal and ruthless. They inspected the factory stores more often and more thoroughly, penalizing even small inaccuracies. They organized raids in the streets and deported people who were rounded up to work in Germany. They blocked streets, making daily and nightly house searches and arrests; and they still hunted fugitives from the ghettos hidden on the Aryan side.

The omniscient Helena informed us when and where a Jew had been found. I learned from her that the Polish police arrested a young couple with a small girl residing in the adjacent house. Later the couple returned home alone and nobody saw the child again. Helena was convinced that she was a Jewish girl because she had heavy eyelids and a terrified facial expression. Her suspicion seemed to have been confirmed. The couple then suddenly disappeared without leaving a forwarding address. Helena had been indignant with them for keeping a Jewish child, and even more so, for doing it in her neighborhood. The question of who had betrayed them did not interest her; she did not see anything wrong in notifying the Germans about hidden Jews.

It was one of many such cases I was told about where the local Polish people helped the Germans in tracking Jews living in Starachowice. Only the Poles were able to detect Semitic characteristics in someone who otherwise looked Aryan. It could be the sad eyes, heavy eyelids, big nose, wide lips, wavy hair, slim hands, skinny legs or countless other details. The Germans were unable to observe the inhabitants of Poland with as much insight as the Poles.

One afternoon the Germans surrounded the small street on which Zdzislaw Slowik lived. He was staying at home at that time because the forest group had been dissolved for the winter and the partisans had returned to their families. Zdzislaw managed to escape and reach our place under the cover of darkness. Nobody knew whom or what the Germans were looking for or why they searched each house on such a side street. Zdzislaw suspected treason in the Underground organization and was afraid it was he whom the Germans wanted. If that was the case, the Germans could next come to us in his pursuit. Dziunia decided that not only Zdzislaw but also I should hide. We both went into the attic over the storage shack and were to stay there until the situation cleared.

The attic was small and low. Long spider webs hung from the ceiling. A lot of straw was spread on the floor. Cold air came in through the wide cracks in the wooden walls. The distant German commands could be heard from time to time in the quiet of the night. I fell asleep very quickly, curled in the corner. Suddenly, Zdzislaw brutally woke me. He tried to take advantage of the fact that we were alone and far away from other family members. My resistance made him wild and ferocious. He aimed his revolver at me, throttled me, beat me in my face, pulled my hair and tore my clothes. Furious, he threatened to denounce me to the Gestapo and slurred me with anti-Semitic epithets. He claimed he had known who I really was for a long time. He seemed to be especially offended that being "only" a Jewess, I did not want him, an Aryan.

Although Zdzislaw held a gun in his hand, I was convinced that he wouldn't use it on me. I fought back. I beat his face and pulled his hair. I was strong and able to defend myself. At dawn, Stasia came to the attic to take her husband home. The Germans finished the search of their street. Apparently, they did not look for Zdzislaw because they stopped the search short of reaching his home.

I returned under Karola's and Dziunia's protective care.

Later, in bed, the question of how Zdzislaw had found out I was a Jewess started to haunt me. He and Stasia were never told this secret. My alibi, worked out with such precision, appeared as weak as the spider web in the attic. I thought about the differences among Karola's children. Dziunia was to me a symbol of what was best and most beautiful in a human being. Her brother proved to be a brutal anti-Semite. I suspected that he would have denounced me to the Germans if not for the deadly consequences for his mother and sister.

The next day, Dziunia asked me if something had happened to me when I was with Zdzislaw in the attic. Although I assured her that everything had been as it should be, she apologized for her brother's behavior.

MARYLA, WHAT SHOULD WE DO?

At the beginning of the spring of 1944, I finished knitting the costume for Karola Slowik. The lined garment was very elegant. Karola looked so beautiful and young in it that she called everybody's attention to herself.

I had great satisfaction looking at this product of my knitting. I wanted this work of many months to reflect the feelings which I was unable to express with words. I had never told Karola Slowik about my enormous gratitude for allowing me to live in her home. It seemed to me that my vocabulary was too poor and my voice too weak. But she somehow understood what I meant to say because whenever she wore the suit, she smiled at me with special warmth. She was very pleased with the garment, claiming that it was the most beautiful piece of clothing she had ever had. She liked to show it to everyone, calling it a masterpiece, praising me so much that I felt embarrassed.

Dzunia wanted to have a similar costume and she had already chosen the color, style and pattern. I would have been very happy to knit it for her, but at that time, we did not have a sufficient quantity of wool. It would take at least half a year to accumulate the necessary amount of rabbit hair. This meant that I would not be able to start knitting before January, 1945. A vision of another year under German occupation was so horrifying that I couldn't even think about this work. But as always, I did not show my anxiety and continued caring for the rabbits.

With the warm days arriving, the routine of our life mirrored that of spring a year ago. Karola started to till the soil in Helena's vegetable garden, assuring herself and the others that this year she would be living back in Lodz before harvesting the fruits of her work. Zdzislaw returned to the partisan squad in the forest. Maria still worked as the liaison officer in the AK (Home Army). Thanks to her, Stasia could receive news about

177

her husband's whereabouts. The AK contact point in our home became very active again. There were different items designated for the partisans and the city organization stored in our attic.

One day, a boy from the neighborhood ran up to us with the news that German cars had appeared on our street. We concluded that the squad of SS was conducting a systematic house-to-house search on Kilinskiego Street. They were at a distance of about half a mile from us and moving in our direction. The Germans' search of our apartment threatened the lives of us all. On that day we were storing approximately 50 pounds of military dry biscuits in a huge sack assigned for the partisans and a pack of illegal newspapers for the local units.

It happened that Dziunia was sick with the flu and stayed in bed. The approach of the Germans and the inevitable search of our apartment threw her off balance. Always brave and calm in the face of danger, now weakened by disease, Dziunia was unable to overcome her fear. She saw no chance for us to survive. Wanting us to be prepared for the awaiting ordeal and death, she told us to pray. She became lost in prayer kneeling in the middle of the kitchen, indifferent to her mother's pleading. Terrified, Karola appealed to me for help. Her words, "Maryla, save Dziunia" touched me to the quick.

I realized that both women were unable to think clearly and that the decision on how to proceed lay exclusively with me. There was some analogy between the present moment and the one preceding my leaving the Konskie Ghetto. Now as then, I was certain that only immediate escape could save me and those closest to me. Now it was Dziunia and Karola; then, Sara and Helenka. I knew I had to hurry. The situation required action instantly.

I told Dziunia and Karola we had to leave home as soon as possible. They did not object. In the meantime, I burned all the illegal newspapers and scattered the ashes in the oven. I moved the heavy sack with the dry biscuits into the darkest place in the attic and covered it with a pile of things. I helped Dziunia and Karola dress and take the most necessary items.

It was very difficult for Karola to leave behind her home and her few precious pre-war possessions saved during her expulsion from Lodz a few years ago. She was also terrified by the danger and the prospect of homelessness. She did not have confidence in her endurance. She was afraid that her poor physical condition would endanger all of us. Suddenly, Karola came up with a new idea. She would stay at home and wait for the SS arrival. Then she would divert their attention from the sack in the attic. She believed the Germans' respect for an elderly woman would save her. She was convinced she was in no danger from them.

Karola's arguments did not convince me. I was certain that if the SS found dry biscuits in an amount sufficient to feed a whole squad of soldiers, her advanced age would not save her. I comprehended how difficult it was for her to leave all that she owned for the second time in the recent past. But I well remembered the fate of those Jews who did not escape to Russia at the beginning of the war because they were unable to separate themselves from what they possessed. I knew the tragic consequences of that. The war experiences taught me not to endanger my life just to save what I owned. Luckily, Dziunia came to my aid and we both categorically refused to leave the apartment without Karola, forcing her to go along with us.

We crossed the backyard and went behind the fence where there was a field covered with young rye. We walked bent so that we could hide in the rye. Whenever we heard voices we laid down on the ground until it was quiet around us again. It was difficult, especially for Karola, to move this way. She complained about back pain as a result of being constantly bent. She was covered with sweat. She often had to stop because she was out of breath. I tried to ease her hardship by

179

taking off her warm coat and all she was carrying. I supported and held her. I appeased, comforted and encouraged her to keep going.

Dzunia, weakened by the illness she had suffered a few days previously, moved with effort. When she had become completely exhausted and couldn't continue to walk, Karola regained strength in a magical way and we both helped Dziunia to go on. Regardless of all these difficulties, we constantly moved farther from our home. The first long rest was when we were already at a substantial distance from our house. After a few hours we reached a part of Starachowice miles away from Kilinskiego Street. There we felt as if we were out of reach of the Germans who had blockaded Kilinskiego Street.

We waited until evening on a path in the field. Then I decided to go to Stasia Slowik and check on the situation. Both Slowik women were exhausted by the many hours of walking and they wanted to rest while waiting for my return. I learned from Stasia that the SS search on Kilinskiego Street had ended some time ago. The Germans had not reached our building, stopping a few houses short of ours. It was safe for us to return home.

Karola became sick after our escape and I felt responsible. The fact that her efforts had been unnecessary deepened my feelings of remorse. Still, I knew that if a similar situation repeated itself, I would again force them to leave home and run away.

Karola and Dziunia did not blame me for the needless escape. On the contrary, the Slowik women showed me even more cordiality and a special confidence. Now they not only asked for my opinion, but in many cases they considered my judgment decisive. Both of them asked me very often, "Maryla, what should we do?" I was flattered by their confidence but I also felt the heaviness of this new responsibility. I lived in constant fear that one day in an unexpected place someone would look at me and cry, "people, she is a Jewess." This fear, hidden from Dziunia and her mother, made me feel as if I were losing my mind. I was afraid that in this mental state, my advice might not be proper. I no longer trusted in my judgment.

One day, the AK (Home Army) authorities asked the Slowik women to shelter a member of the organization in their home for a short time. The place where he had stayed was "burned out" (became known to the Germans). In this emergency he needed a new refuge immediately. Dziunia and her mother were inclined to accept the unknown man. When they asked me the usual question, "Maryla, what should we do?" I suggested we use his temporary sojourn with us to strengthen my alibi among the neighbors. We decided that this stranger would come to us as my visiting brother. Thanks to such an arrangement, I would receive confirmation of my assumed biography and he a safe place to stay.

Similarly, as in the past when I had advertised my mother's arrival, I now told everyone about my brother's expected visit. But this time I was certain "my sibling" would arrive. One evening a young man knocked at our door and introduced himself as Jerzy Czajkowski. He assumed my last name, as we had suggested.

My newly created brother was of medium height with dark blond hair, light eyes and the pleasant, smiling face of a big boy. He was nineteen years old, exactly my age although he looked much younger. We decided to present him as two years younger. In the evening, I introduced him to many elements of my Aryan biography known to the neighbors. He happened to be a willing and capable student. He absorbed all the information without asking unnecessary questions.

Jerzy, our new tenant, took my bed in the kitchen. I slept on a straw mattress in the room with Dziunia and Karola. He was a more mature person than one would suspect judging from his childish appearance. Jerzy was polite, intelligent and well-read. He easily established contact with our neighbors who liked him at first sight. I received many compliments on my brother's behavior. Some neighbors found a lot of similarities in the two of us.

Jerzy tried to help me in the household duties. Now it was he who carried water up and down the stairs, made a fire in the oven and chopped wood for the winter. In the evenings we talked about the books we had read in the past and discussed some of them. We never touched the subject of our private lives before the war. Although Jerzy lived together with us in one small apartment, we did not know his true name or from where he had come. He was grateful for the shelter and acceptance from the Slowik's family, showing his gratitude not only to Karola and Dziunia, but also to me.

The constant presence of Jerzy awakened a nostalgia for my true brother. He had sent letters from the City of Rowne until the outbreak of the Russian-German war. In June of 1941 this connection had ceased to exist. We did not hear from or about him anymore. I deeply believed that he had escaped into Russia, far away from the Germans' power. I thought and dreamed about him often. In these dreams we were together with our father in our pre-war apartment in Konskie.

During the few weeks my Polish brother stayed with us, I felt much more secure than before. I had the impression that he protected me from suspicious glances and hatred toward Jews. In his presence the chronic feeling of fear weakened and my loneliness in the Polish world was less painful. I was grateful to him for all of that but obviously couldn't show him my feelings.

One evening a man came to take him away. We said goodbye very warmly, as if we were true siblings. I thought I saw sadness underneath his always smiling eyes.

APPROACHING LIBERATION

Very favorable news from the Eastern Front reached us at the beginning of summer, 1944. The Soviet Army moved westward with unprecedented speed, liberating city after city. By now it was obvious to me that the German defeat must happen within a very short time. The underground newspaper announced that the Soviet Army had crossed the pre-war Polish frontiers in many places. The distance from the Eastern Front to Starachowice became shorter every day.

The appearance of the soldiers in the German Army had changed completely. Older men had replaced the young soldiers in the transports sent from the west to the east. They did not resemble the victorious and enthusiastic German conquerors who had passed in the same direction three years ago. They looked tired and indifferent. Many trains of wounded soldiers returned from the east. They often stopped at the Starachowice station. It was easy to see what a terrible state the defeated Germans were in.

One evening, sirens hooted for the first time since I had been in Starachowice, announcing the approach of an air attack. The alarm publicly and loudly proclaimed the appearance of the enemy of German power. The sound of sirens made me happy and brave. In defiance of German prohibitions I did not want to hide in the basement or even remain indoors. I had to go out. I couldn't refuse myself the pleasure of seeing the bombardment directed against the Germans, even if it could be dangerous. I went through the fence and lay down on the ground in the field.

As if in a magical theater, extraordinary events took place in the air. At first I heard the very strange noise of an engine drawing nearer and nearer. Then I saw an airplane with a huge red star. The loud machine flew so low that I could see the Soviet pilot wearing large protective glasses. Suddenly, almost directly above me, glittered a ball like a gigantic lamp hanging directly in the air. It lit Starachowice as if a sunny day had replaced the darkness of the night. It seemed to me that in this light everything became visible to the Soviet pilot. The thought that he could also see me lying in the field gave me a feeling of direct contact with him.

Meanwhile, more Soviet planes crowded the sky. I saw the falling bombs and heard explosions close-by. I felt the trembling of the earth and saw a fire in the center of Starachowice where the munitions factory was. I felt no fear of the bombardment although I found myself in the middle of an air fight. I witnessed something that I had dreamed about throughout all the years of war. I was fascinated by this miraculous occurrence - an attack on the Germans.

Then the air defense started. The German bullets against the Soviet planes left behind lines of lights in the air. They did not reach the attackers. The planes with red stars returned home without any damage that evening. I said goodbye to them feeling gratitude as if the Soviet pilot had come to Starachowice especially for me. Until now the Germans attacked and conquered country after country. They were able to suppress resistance on the ground, on the sea and in the air. They were always victorious. Finally I had seen them weak unable to defend themselves.

The war against the Germans took place in front of my eyes and no longer in some abstract part of the world. Now I believed that the army which would liberate me was close. I could be free soon from the stigma of being a Jew, the death sentence and from all the Germans.

For the next days and weeks, the air attacks were frequent. Mostly during the night, the sirens of the approaching air raid sent us downstairs where all the neighbors had gathered. After I had found a place for Karola, I went outside. I wanted to observe the air strikes. I felt as if I took part in the attack just by looking at it. It seemed like "my fight" against the Germans. Dziunia seldom joined my adventure. She seemed to feel safer staying with her mother inside the walls of the house.

One night the sounds of gunshots awakened me; they lasted for several hours. Later the distant sounds, heard at first only in the silence of the night, became closer and louder. After a few days I could also hear them clearly during the day. There had been a battle east of Starachowice and the gunfire had come from there.

Stanislaw brought the information that the Soviet Army was approaching the Vistula River approximately 60 miles away from us. Small Soviet scout squads appeared in a few neighboring towns. They disappeared very quickly, clearly avoiding a confrontation with the enemy. The Germans were visibly in a state of panic. They had taken the arms factory apart and sent it west. Departing German families crowded the train station in Starachowice. All the signs on the ground and in the sky indicated the liberation would reach us no later than in a few days. However, the Germans did not loosen their grip. On the contrary, they simultaneously intensified the terror. Poles were being arrested on the streets, at homes, in the work places and forcibly sent to the factories as slave workers. More and more often, the Germans surrounded whole blocks of the city and transported the people rounded up to Germany.

Dziunia stopped going to work. We introduced twenty-four hour watches at the open window overlooking Kilinskiego Street. During the night vigils, I listened to any suspicious sound and looked for any sign of dubious movement. We were now always on alert and ready to run away if the Germans would appear in our neighborhood. While watching the dark street, I thought that if the Germans suddenly surrounded our house simultaneously from all sides we would not be able to escape across the courtyard. I took into my head the idea of creating a hiding place in our house similar to the ones built in the Ghetto. However, I did not know how to realize this plan.

We learned that the Polish uprising started on August 1,

1944 in Warsaw. At the same time the Soviet army had entered Praga – the Warsaw borough – on the east side of the Vistula River. Enormous happiness overcame all the population. The Polish compatriots had finally taken the task of freeing Warsaw into their own hands, ending the passive wait for the liberation. Now the Polish people fought openly against the Germans to free their capital. All the inhabitants of our house were very proud of the heroism of "our boys " and showed their enthusiasm and moral support. There was an outburst of patriotism among all the neighbors. They walked from one apartment to another with congratulations and wishes for a speedy victory. There was an atmosphere of festivity in the air. Stanislaw took out a camera hidden for many years and took pictures of everyone to memorialize "the last days of the war on Kilinskiego Street". He photographed Karola, Dziunia, Stasia with Alinka and me with some neighbors in Helena's garden full of flowers.

During these happy days, Dziunia gave me her picture with the beautiful dedication, "To dear Maryla for a keepsake. From the wartime – a time of terrible suffering. Your sister, Dziunia. Starachowice, August 17, 1944."

Karola also offered me her photograph. She wrote with hands shaking from excitement, "To dear Maryla, as proof of my warm feeling and attachment which will remain always the same. Your aunt, Karola."

The news of Warsaw Uprising made me happy. I followed all the news coming from the fighting field in the capital with great interest. I shared with the Polish insurgents their successes. I felt my affiliation with the Polish nation very strongly in those days, despite a general belief that the Jews were not Polish patriots.

I also thought about the Jewish uprising which had broken out in the same city one year ago. Most of the people I knew did not consider the Jewish fighters heroes. The same neighbors who were full of patriotic feelings and admiration for the Polish insurgents had scoffed at the Jewish ones and repeated anti-Semitic slogans. With sadness, I thought about the young Jews who died lonely deaths fighting against the Germans without any hope of victory. Their heroism did not result in pride or respect by the Poles although they had fought under the Polish white/red national flag. Their struggle evoked no recognition in the Polish world even after the collapse of the uprising.

One night I realized that there was silence in the air. The gunfire had stilled. No air raids awakened me. There was no bombardment of Starachowice. The Soviet Army had halted at the Vistula River. This shocking news was too tragic for me to accept. I deceived myself that the inertness of the liberating army would be of a short duration. I still expected the Soviets to resume their attacks and march west at any moment. I waited for the sound of sirens and falling bombs every night. Each day I expected the Soviets to enter Starachowice. But time was passing and the Eastern front did not move on. The Soviets did not resume their fight with the Germans. They were still on the east shore of the Vistula River.

I thought a lot about Sara and Helenka. Until now Stanislaw would bring me some information about them from time to time. I knew that they had lived in a small settlement near the Vistula River. This part of Poland had been recaptured by the Soviets during this summer offensive. Thus they were free by now if they had survived the Soviet attack and the German defense. However, all connection with the part of Poland east of the Vistula River ceased to exist and I did not expect any information about them any longer. (1)

One day we learned about the collapse of the Warsaw Uprising. The Polish fighters had surrendered and were taken prisoner. The Germans forced all the Warsaw inhabitants to abandon the city. The Soviets continued to stay in Praga, the eastern district of Warsaw. Refugees from Warsaw, different in many ways from the local people, appeared on the streets of

Starachowice. They were the witnesses to the end of the uprising and the total destruction of Warsaw, the capital of Poland. The Germans had razed Warsaw to the ground.

A general sadness replaced the recent joy. A feeling of hopelessness and disappointment supplanted the euphoria of victory. A feeling of national mourning overwhelmed everyone. Dziunia and her mother were painfully touched by the fall of the Warsaw Uprising. They both lost hope and energy. Dziunia became ill suffering from stomach aches.

I was also upset by the defeat of the Warsaw Insurgence and by the destruction of the beautiful city Warsaw had been. I did not understand the silence and stillness on the Eastern Front. The word "treason" was repeated in most conversations. Even Stanislaw, who was always well informed about politics, couldn't explain the present situation. Why did the Soviets halt at the river shore after the fast, victorious march west? Why didn't they prevent the defeat of the Polish uprising? These questions were left without a response. My liberation stopped with the Soviets.

The victories of the Allied Army at the Western front did not soften my grief. I listened without any enthusiasm to the news that the Americans and the British had landed in France and liberated the capitals of Belgium and Holland. These victorious Allied advances were too far away. Close to me, at a distance of a couple of days of marching, was the motionless Soviet Army. The Germans in Starachowice returned to governing by force and terror after the temporary panic caused by the closeness of the Russians. The number of daily and night raids on the Polish population increased.

Dziunia again started to go to work regularly in what was left of the arms factory. I resumed the daily household duties. Anxiety was with me all the time, day and night. I tortured myself again with the conviction that the Germans would kill me in the last moment of their rule. Often I watched Kilinskiego Street for many hours in the darkness of the night.

I knew that we were very vulnerable if the Germans came. The thought about building an appropriate hiding place was always on my mind.

I convinced Dziunia and Karola that we should have a secret room in case of the sudden surrounding of our house by the Germans. We tried to find a suitable space for it and we very carefully checked the kitchen, bedroom and both attics. We were unable to find one. I came to the conclusion that we should include all the tenants of the house in our plan and together find the right solution. As a result of my insistence, Dziunia convinced the neighbors about the necessity of having a hiding place for the people in danger. All the men and young women belonged to that category. Stanislaw, excited by our initiative, immediately started its realization.

In the autumn of 1944, the secret room under our house was built, thanks to a combined effort of almost all the tenants. An underground passage from the cellar below the kitchen floor under the Pragas' apartment led to the hiding place. This corridor, a few meters long, was low and required crawling through it. The secret space was at the end of this passage. It had a constant flow of fresh air coming through an opening created by a few missing bricks in the wall. This underground room could accommodate approximately ten persons lying close to each other. Although the entrance to this place was in the Praga's apartment, everyone had the right to use it in case of danger.

My plan had been realized. There was a good hiding place in our house. The thought that I could find refuge there when it would be needed helped me to survive each of the following difficult days.

_____

(1) Sara and Helenka survived the war . A few years later, Sara married again. She emigrated with her husband and Helenka to Israel at the end of the 1940s. She died there as Sara Ponczek in 1989. Helenka lives in Israel with her husband, children and grandchildren.

The number of different partisan groups in the neighborhood of Starachowice increased significantly in the autumn of 1944. The most popular underground network in the city and forest was AK (Home Army). Dziunia, her siblings and almost all of the Slowik's acquaintances collaborated with this organization to a smaller or greater degree. However, more and more often, I learned about the attacks on the Germans by the AL (People's Army) (1). Moreover, the Soviet guerilla fighters made themselves noticeable especially in the nearby woods. Some terrorist actions were conducted by NSZ (National Armed Forces). This organization directed its attacks against the Germans as well as the Soviet partisans.

At the end of 1944, all these resistance movements intensified the fight against the occupying forces. The partisans blew up train tracks, disarmed German military squads, attacked supply depots and enforced the verdicts of their military courts by punishing collaboration with the enemy.

At the same time, German repressive measures increased in Starachowice and in the surroundings. Their forces penetrated the forest and attacked the partisan groups in their camps. During one such action the Germans surrounded and destroyed the partisan squad I had been a part of the previous year. "Grot", the commander, and all the partisans present in the camp perished in the fight. Zdzislaw Slowik survived. Thanks to a lucky coincidence, he was in another place at that time.

The death of these partisans was painful to me. The time of brotherhood we spent together made me feel close to them. They were mostly young idealists, full of enthusiasm, dedicated to the cause of their homeland. They were friendly and protective of me. But I did not have a chance to learn how they would have treated me had they known I was Jewish.

Zdzislaw left the forest after the loss of his comrades-in-arms. He decided to stay with his wife at least during the approaching winter months. Because his apartment was close to our home, the hiding space beneath our house also became a place of safety for him.

At this time, together with a few neighbors, I took part in the night vigils outside the house or at the window facing the street. Several times the Germans appeared on our street at midnight and once even surrounded the adjoining house. People who had been on watch alerted all the tenants about the potential danger. Dziunia and I had covered up our tracks in the apartment and ran to the Pragas' cellar. Karola stayed at home. She refused to hide underground.

One afternoon, when Dziunia was still at work, several German cars arrived at our house and stopped at the gate. No one noticed them for some time because our observatory network was active only at night. Suddenly, I heard German voices and saw a group of them in our garden. I was terrified by this unexpected closeness of the German uniforms. I immediately notified the whole house and went into the hiding place together with Stanislaw and Wanda. Karola and Mrs. Praga closed the entrance to the cellar behind us and both of them returned to their apartments. We lay in the low, musty underground without any movement for many hours waiting for a sign that it was safe to come out.

When we were finally let out from hiding, we found out that the Germans had sized one room for their officer in the front apartment in our house. No one knew why they had chosen this particular place located far way from the center of the city or how they had learned about this apartment. The nightly return of the Germans, the sudden grating sound of the cars' brakes, the loud German language under my window awakened me often and caused uncontrollable dread. I was not able to distinguish these "peacefully" oriented German neighbors from their countrymen who always threatened my life. The presence of the Germans in the vicinity paralyzed our alarm system. Their constant traffic hindered the discovery of a true threat.

Successful hiding under such conditions would be impossible.

A few days later, Zofia, the owner of the front apartment, notified Dziunia that her German occupant had shown an alarming curiosity in all the tenants of our house. This news bothered me. I tried to keep to our apartment, especially when the car in front of the house indicated the presence of the German officer. Zdzislaw stopped visiting his mother and sister and his wife became the only family link. The AK, informed about our situation, temporarily closed the point of contact in our home. Stanislaw decided to leave Starachowice and join the partisans even though winter was approaching. I thought about going with him and joining the forest army. I asked Stanislaw to arrange my admittance to the same unit that he was joining, but he was unable to do it. The partisan group refused to admit a girl not previously engaged in their underground work .

One day Stanislaw said goodbye. Together with his comrades, he planned to reach the Soviet Army entrenched at the other side of the Vistula River. In order to achieve this goal they had to go through the German line of defense. They took this risk. Stanislaw had been my confidant and friend. It was painful for me to see him leave. I never again heard from or about him. He disappeared forever for me.

I received a cigarette as Stanislaw's goodbye gift. "Smoke it when you feel down," he advised me. He thought smoking effectively cured tension. He always hid his smoking from Helena. I had learned about his habit some time before. When we were alone he liked to treat me to a cigarette.

One night, when everyone was already asleep and I restlessly lay with open eyes for many long hours, I decided to reach for this cigarette. Stanislaw was right. Smoking helped me fall asleep. I was awakened by Karola's very nervous voice. She claimed that a man had been someplace in our home. We both very carefully searched all the dark places and corners in our apartment, but we found no one. Later I realized that the smell of my burning cigarette caused Karola's association with the presence of a man. However, I was too embarrassed to admit to my smoking.

I turned twenty years old in November. Obviously, no one in my surroundings knew about my birthday. I left my true identity in the Ghetto when I escaped. I left it with the nine thousand Jews who had lived there. I had lost myself there together with all the Jews in Konskie. During my birthday, lying sleepless in the bed, I indulged myself in wandering through my past. The pictures from the pre-war years seemed to be so unreal that they resembled a fairy tale. I had lived a beautiful life in the past, I thought.

Reminiscing about my father evoked very strong feelings of the love I always had for him. I saw his head with short gray hair, pale face, golden-brown eyes under thick eyebrows. I recalled him being dressed in a white coat in the office or walking in the evenings with a cane and hat or sitting at the table in our dining room filled with black furniture. I imagined him calling me by my pet name "Halutka", which only he used. I remembered his favorite songs from the Moniuszko's opera "Halka". I heard him sing, almost without any melody, the popular hit "The Town of Belz". I pictured him as he checked my homework, corrected my Polish essays, helped me draw the map for geography class and questioned me about the capitals of the European countries. In front of my eyes I had the image of him when he was healthy, full of happiness, laughing and joking. I saw him also when he cried after his brother was murdered by the Germans. (2)

I recalled my father when he became very sick and I felt pain caused by my complete hopelessness in fighting his progressive disease. I thought about his death in June of 1942. For the first time, I considered it to be a blessing. He was able to die in his own bed, surrounded by his family. His Polish friends and the inhabitants of the Konskie Ghetto still had the opportunity to honor his human dignity by attending his funeral and burying and burying him in the cemetery. He was spared the terrible end awaiting all the other Jews.

In some gruesome way my father's death made it possible for me to escape from the Ghetto. I knew he would not have abandoned the people close to him. He would have remained with them until the end. I was convinced that if he were alive, I could not have left him alone at that dangerous time and place. The thought that his death made me somehow alive became a new tie binding me to the memory of my beloved father.

The birthday recollections brought me more pain than pleasure. Only the hope that Sara, Helenka and my brother Jerzy thought about me on this day and wished me to survive the war was some consolation.

During the months of autumn and winter of 1944 we started to experience difficulties with food supplies. The Germans significantly decreased the rations while increasing the control-system for distributed products. Dziunia, though very resourceful and brave, was now unable to help herself and her friends as much as before.

The brothers Adams and Jan (3) belonged to the people whom Dziunia had continuously helped for more than a year. Irena, the officer of the AK organization had personally asked for it. She told Dziunia both brothers were involved in the underground to such an extent that they were unable to support themselves and their closest families. Dziunia learned that Adam and Jan were high officers in the NSZ (National Armed Forces) unit in Starachowice.

During the past year, Adam and Jan had tried to come into social contact with the Slowik family. Dziunia, knowing the anti-Semitic character of the organization they belonged to, did not want to socialize with them. She refused many of their invitations under different pretenses. However, when she finally ran short of excuses she yielded to their persistent persuasion. One day, Dziunia and her mother paid a visit to

Adam and Jan. The evening with the new acquaintances was pleasant and the atmosphere in the hosts's home very warm. Dziunia claimed the time spent there was a nice diversion from the monotonous, everyday life. They learned from the brothers that he Allied Army had already entered into German territory. In view of such an important occurrence, the fact the Soviet Army had not moved ahead for the last several months seemed less important.

After the first visit, the social contact with the brothers became more frequent. Dziunia and Karola did not mind going there anymore. During each visit the hosts asked about me. They always expressed regret because of my absence and renewed the invitation. After several encounters Dziunia decided that my further refusal could create dangerous suspicions. Thus, one Sunday afternoon the three of us paid a visit to Adam and Jan.

They lived in a small house in the center of Starachowice. We were received very warmly. The brothers and their wives did not have enough words of gratitude for Dziunia. They considered her a person sent by Providence to help them. The visit turned out to be a pleasant event even for me. I was entertained by interesting and amusing stories. The hosts clearly tried to make me feel comfortable and enjoy the time spent in their home. The warm atmosphere allowed me to forget about the brothers' affiliation with a fascist organization. I even started to see it as impossible that these intelligent and friendly people could have a murderous approach toward the Jews.

Adam and Jan's hatred toward all Jews became visible in full its intensity during the next meeting. They considered all members of the Jewish nation as the most dangerous enemies of Poland. They completely approved of the extermination of Jews conducted by the Germans. In their house, I again heard the very well-known expression about the monument for Hitler being a token of gratitude for cleansing the homeland of Jews.

During the first few contacts with the brothers I was able to control my conscious and unconscious reactions to their anti-Semitic attacks. However, each consecutive visit magnified my nervousness and debilitated my inner defense system. I felt sick to my stomach listening to their talk. Then a wave of heat would pass through my body. The red spots on my face and my neck were visible symptoms of what was going on within me.

I found myself in a very difficult situation. I did not know how I could counteract this danger which intensified and tightened around me. I could not stop the visits now and I could not control my reaction to their hatred of Jews anymore. The only thing left for me was to camouflage the red patches on my face as effectively as was possible. I started to use all the tricks I had practiced for the last two years which had worked for me until then. I threw something on the floor and looked for it until the redness disappeared from the face. I pretended to have an attack of coughing or a sudden need to go to the toilet.

One evening, with dread, I realized that Adam and Jan had seen through me. I caught their shock and anger caused by their startling discovery. They realized what had made me blush. Both brothers immediately began skillful questioning as if it were a police interrogation. Although now I could answer their deceitful questions calmly and even jokingly, I knew it was too late. They already were convinced I was Jewish. All of this happened in a room full of people. Dziunia and Karola, unaware of the situation, were having a nice conversation with the other guests a few steps away from me. All of a sudden, it occurred to me that my foreboding, according to which I would die at the very end of the war, had come true. The only comforting thought I had was that the NSZ organization would not dare to harm Dziunia and Karola.

Shortly after this visit, Irena came to us as an official representative of the AK in Starachowice. She informed us that this organization would discontinue all contact with the Slowiks because they had hidden a Jew in their home. Helena Kostrzewa, the owner of our house, had also been notified about me at the same time. She stopped talking to Dziunia and ostentatiously turned her head away whenever I was in sight.

A few days later, I went to fetch water from the well. As I turned homeward with the full bucket, I saw Adam barring me from the way home. His face and eyes expressed such hatred that I became paralyzed by fear. I was convinced that it was my last moment. and now he would kill me.

"We kill Jews," he started to talk slowly and clearly, "with a clean conscience because the future of Poland requires it. The same fate might be yours. Only because of Dziunia are we sparing your life for now. However, if you should betray us or our organization, no force will be able to save you."

Adam turned and very quickly left the courtyard. A slam of the gate resounded like a gun shot.

It was December of 1944.

---

(1) AL (Armia Ludowa – People's Army) was a military underground organization which combined People's Guard and other communist and socialist fighting battalions.

(2) Szymon Kon, born in 1885 in Warsaw, was murdered in 1941.

(3) Adam and Jan are fictional names – I have forgotten their true ones.

I SURVIVED THE GERMANS

At the beginning of 1945, the Germans still reigned supreme in Starachowice and in the whole western part of Poland. All the rumors that the Eastern front had moved westward from the shore of the Vistula River, that many neighboring towns had been liberated by Soviet paratroopers, always turned out false. The local reliable source categorically stated that the Soviet Army had remained for the last few months in the same place about 50 miles from Starachowice.

In the summer of 1944, I believed that only days separated me from the liberation. The Russians were coming closer and closer to us each day then. When they suddenly stopped at the Vistula River, I expected them to move forward after only a short rest and reorganization for a week or two at the most. Now six months had passed and the position of the Eastern Front remaining unchanged. I lost the hope of being free any time soon. I even came to the painful conclusion that the present front line in the vicinity of Starachowice must be the ultimate border of the Soviet expansion to the west.

Meanwhile, in spite of the quietness at the Eastern Front, the Germans again displayed some clear unrest. They completely closed down the production of arms and sent the remaining machinery to Germany. There was a rumor they had recently mined the munitions factory, the power station and of many others buildings utilized by them for production and offices. The terrified inhabitants of Starachowice were convinced that half of the city would be blown up at the time of the Germans' ultimate departure. Mass arrests and forced deportations to work in Germany were also associated with the Germans' preparation to leave the city.

Dziunia, like all the workers of the munitions factory, lost her job. We were glad that her days of constant danger at work were over and she could stay at home with us.

One afternoon in the middle of January, I unexpectedly

noticed a squad of Germans marching along Kilinskiego Street. The first ranks of the military force passed our house hastening toward the nearest forest. Standing hidden behind the curtain, I tried to estimate the size of this military unit. I saw our street in all its visible length covered by the columns of the Germans. Time passed, but the numerous lines of soldiers with their full military equipment marched and marched on in front of the window. Our street was not a big throughway. On the contrary, it was a sandy road leading only to the surrounding villages and hamlets. The presence of the huge German infantry on their way into the forest was very puzzling. The size of this military unit and the speed of its movement ruled out a blockade of our part of the city. The first lines of this army must have already been on the empty road in the woods, well beyond the border of the city. I did not stop watching the marching columns of German infantry. The alarmed neighbors bolted their doors, barring the entrances to their houses. Dziunia and I were ready to hide underground whenever it would be necessary.

A few hours passed and nothing changed until the evening, when the marching army suddenly stopped. A dozen or so soldiers entered our garden and a moment later started to rattle at the main entrance. Then Dziunia, some neighbors and I ran into our hiding place. Karola and the other older people decided to remain in their apartments.

The darkness in the underground space was so deep that I was unable to see Dziunia although she was lying near me. I constantly checked on her presence as if I were afraid to lose her. In the silence I heard the throbbing of my own heart and the accelerated breathing of the people around me. I felt the dense, wet air covering my body. Then I heard loud German words coming from the courtyard, blows to the door and the sound of heavy steps inside the house. The wooden support above my head started to shake. I knew the Germans were on the ground floor in the Pragas' apartment. I tried not to imagine what they were doing there. The noise and traffic lasted for an hour.

After that, silence was in the house and in the courtyard for a short time. Then again, there were German shouts, blows to the door and sounds of heavy military steps all over the house. The cycle repeated many times during that long night.

At dawn, we were notified that the danger had passed. The march of the German infantry along our street lasted about twelve hours. Every few hours the army stopped for a short break. The soldiers who were close to our house demanded to be let inside under the threat of guns. The Germans insisted on receiving food and drink. Even though they did not always get something to eat, they harmed no one. Luckily, they did not enter our apartment on the second floor where Karola stayed on guard all night.

There was a silence when I left the underground hiding place. Numerous footprints were all over the sandy road in front of our house.

I slept quite a long time after the stressful, wakeful night. When I later went outside to fetch water, the bright sun blinded my eyes. It was a beautiful, frosty day – January 19, 1945.

I noticed a boy surrounded by the neighbors. I knew him well. He and his older sister used to come to us often. Dziunia had provided them with food for as long as I could remember. I was surprised to see the excitement he had created among the grownups. All the people were talking to the boy at the same time. He clearly was glad to see me as if I had come to his rescue. He looked for my appreciation which he had not found among the listeners. He immediately started to explain to me what had happened.

"None of them believe me. I swear to God, I am telling the truth. There are Russians in the city. There are a lot of them riding on huge tanks. They are different from the Germans. I saw them myself. My sister ordered me to run to Miss Dziunia and tell her about it."

At first, the boy's words did not reach my consciousness. He must have noticed my indifference because he kept convincing me that he was talking about things he himself had just witnessed. Suddenly, my head started reeling so fast that I had to catch hold of the boy to protect myself from falling down. I left the conversing group without a word and went upstairs. I felt weak. My legs quivered as I walked. I repeated to Dziunia and Karola what the boy had said. I heard myself telling the news but my voice sounded strange to me as if it were not mine. My head spun again. I had to sit in order not to lose my balance. I felt odd, not myself.

In spite of my physical weakness, I decided to go to the center of the city and check if the Soviets were really there.

Both women tried to convince me not to go. They reminded me of many instances when similar information had been false. They urged me to be cautious and wait in the safety of our home for confirmation of the news. They warned me against danger from front-line soldiers if Russians really had entered the city. They wanted me to stay with them patiently.

Listening to them I knew that I would be unable to do what they asked. I felt as if I could not go through another disappointment and one additional hour of uncertainty. I was unable to accept any longer the thought that the boy's story was false. It seemed to me that in the last few minutes I had lost all my physical and mental endurance. I had to see my liberators for myself and be close to them. I had to watch their steps and not let them leave me behind. I must not allow them to give me back to the Germans.

Suddenly, unexpectedly, I started to weep. Uncontrollable sobs shook my whole body. Tears rolled down my face. They blocked and choked my breath. Crying, a natural human impulse, impossible for me for many years, now completely overwhelmed me.

Both women were surprised and terrified by my strange reaction. During the two years they had lived with me, they had not seen a single tear on my face. They probably suspected I was unable to cry. Feeling helpless, they did not object any longer to my trip to the city.

I walked along empty streets toward the center of Starachowice. I moved faster and faster. I started to run as if I were pushed ahead by some unseen force. I kept tripping against the stones protruding from the snow. I slipped on the icy road. Tears obscured my vision. Sobs hindered my breathing. I felt increasing weakness in my legs. I was afraid that I would not have enough strength to reach my goal.

At the crossroads of Kilinskiego Street and the one leading from Ostrowiec to Skarzysko, I stopped, petrified. An uninterrupted river of people and steel flowed a few steps from me. Gigantic tanks, armored cars, guns, iron machines and enormous numbers of soldiers moved westward. The huge army completely covered the pavement.

The scene I looked at was no illusion, no dream. It had really happened. The Soviets were there at a distance of a few feet from me. I could take another step or two and touch the soldiers with my own hands. I could hear scraps of their conversation and the words of strange songs in the rumble of the tanks. I could breathe the hot air coming from their vehicles.

I took in the view of soldiers and war engines passing by. I could not appease my hunger for this sight. It was a treat to my eyes and my mind. Very slowly, I realized the simple fact that if the Russians were in Starachowice, the Germans had deserted this city. The magnitude of that logic started to reach my consciousness. The Russians had freed me from the death penalty and restored my right to life. They gave me back my human dignity. I realized that I had survived the Germans. This awareness evoked in me enormous loneliness. I felt pain for my lost people and my unique world. I found myself in an emptiness surrounded by hostile strangers. I started to cry again.

203

I stood on the empty sidewalk near the constantly moving Soviet Army. I was motionless at the shore of a river pressing westward. I was not aware of time passing. I did not feel the cold penetrating my whole body.

Dzunia found me there late in the evening and forced me to return home.

SOME YEARS LATER

It was close to 9:00 p.m. when I left the laboratory. A cold breeze on the street was refreshing after hours of breathing the fumes of the solvents in an overcrowded room. The street was empty. No pedestrians on the sidewalks and no vehicles on the pavement. Quiet reigned around me. It was a pleasant change after the noise of the stuffy laboratory.

I was teaching chemistry at the University of Lodz to third year students (1). On this particular day, the class on experimental organic synthesis, took place in a temporary laboratory. Its space was poorly adapted to this kind of chemical experimentation and the number of students. The danger of an accident such as fire or burns was probable in this crowd of young and inexperienced chemists. The difficult conditions made me tense during the class and extremely exhausted when it ended.

I was very glad when the last student had left the laboratory and I was able to close the door behind him. Although it was late and I was tired, I decided to walk home. Strolling along the poorly lit Buczka Street, I became completely lost in my thoughts.

Unexpectedly, I found myself in a ring of light. The crossroad of the three streets: Buczka, Jaracza and Uniwersytecka was brightened by the glaring light. The luminosity of this intersection contrasted enormously with the darkness of all the crossing streets. I felt as if I were transferred from a deep night to sunny noon in a single, magic moment. I stopped and looked around for the source of this unusual and unexpected occurrence. A few street lamps and several big bright store windows lightened the corner.

Surprised, I couldn't understand why I had not noticed this shopping center before, which was so conveniently situated near my workplace. I was curious what kind of articles were being sold in these new stores. Big loaves of bread, round and crescent rolls, cakes and various cookies lay decoratively arranged. Above the window display was the owner's name and the sign "bakery' in big letters. A long while passed before I realized I had automatically translated what I had read. In fact, the sign read not the word "bakery" but its German equivalent, *"Backerei"*. A note in German placed at eye level stated that Jews and dogs were forbidden entry into this store.

The adjoining shop also had a big and bright window display. Here, around a porcelain pig, pieces of fresh looking meat, ham, sausages and various cold cuts were lying. The sign informed me that meat was being sold at certain hours of the day but only to Germans.

I was bewildered. I looked around for someone to explain to me what I had just seen. I felt a growing anxiety in me. I did not want to be alone at this moment. I desperately needed somebody to be with me. But as far as I could see, not a single person was on the three cross streets. The whole neighborhood looked deserted. It seemed to me that I had lost my orientation and found myself in an unknown place. Where was I? Trying to clear my mind, I approached the sign with the name of the street. *"Adolf Hitler Strasse"* (Adolf Hitler Street), I read over and over again.

I was seized by horror and panic. I felt a buzzing in my head and nausea in my throat. I did not understand what was happening. I could not comprehend the situation. I did not know what the present time was.

I found only one logical explanation: The Second World War still was going on. The Germans continued to occupy Poland and they ruled according to their criminal laws. I would have to incessantly hide my Jewishness while a death sentence hung over my head. That seemed to be the reality. Everything else was the work of my wishful imagination and my hallucinations. Only in my dreams had I survived the war, finished my university studies, started a family and baby son was waiting for me at home. I sat on the curb of the sidewalk lit by street lamps and shop windows. I was losing my strength. I felt as if my body was drooping and dying. I curled up and closed my eyes.

"Don't you feel well?" Unexpectedly, I heard a male voice above me. I looked up and saw a Polish policeman near me.

"Officer," I turned to him "what year is it now?"

"What happened to you? You seem to be sick. I could take you to the hospital close by," the policeman kept asking.

"Tell me please what year is it? What is the date today?" I insisted on the answer to my questions, hoping that this particular piece of information would clarify everything.

"1956," he answered and started to check the contents of my handbag which he had lifted from the ground. "Mrs. Zawadzka, you are residing at Wieckowkiego Street in Lodz. You are teaching at the University of Lodz..." The policeman read my documents loudly.

"Tell me if the war is still on?" I interrupted him.

"No, it ended a long time ago."

"And this," I pointed at the brightly lit store windows at the crossing.

"This is just a model of a street from the time of the Second World War. A film will be made about that period. Why did these German stores frighten you so much?" The policeman looked sincerely surprised.

His words allowed me to rouse myself from my state of terror. I stood up with the help of the policeman. We walked together. He wanted to see me off to the nearest streetcar stop. Slowly, I was recovering from the shock which had hit me so violently. I was thinking about what had just happened. I was asking myself when the injuries left by the years of hiding would start to heal. When would I get rid of the fear which awakened me suddenly from sleep? When would I get rid of the feeling of choking when someone's gaze stopped a little too long on me? When would I cease to pretend to be someone else? When would I have the luxury of being myself?

Maybe then I would not be frightened to death by German stores and signs.

At the streetcar stop, the policeman asked me once more why I had feared the film scenery.

"I am a Jewess," I answered. I saw first surprise and then embarrassment on his face.

"You don't look like one," he said.

I knew that he wanted to please me by this goodbye compliment.

---

(1) The described event took place probably in 1956.

EPILOGUE

During the first twenty-five years after the Second World War, I built my new existence on the ruins left by the Germans. I tried to block the memories of my tragic past and live a normal life. However, in spite of my attempts, I was not always in control of my feelings and emotions. I constantly had recurrent nightmares in which I ran away, had been caught, hid in dark corners, unsuccessfully looked for a shelter and again ran away. . . I still had an uncontrollable physiological reaction to hearing words of hatred toward the Jews.

I settled in the City of Lodz where Karola and Dziunia Slowik returned with their family. At the beginning of 1946, Dziunia died after a very short illness at the age of thirty-nine. She remains in my memory as one of the most beautiful human beings I have known.

Soon after the war, I went back to school. In the following years, I graduated from high school and the University of Lodz, consecutively with Master and Doctor of Sciences degrees. I was offered a research and teaching position at the Department of Organic Chemistry at the University of Lodz. Gradually I moved up the ladder of promotions to the position of Associate Professor. I started a family, had a son, friends and a job I liked.

I knew that the system in Poland was far from perfect and many times I was painfully disappointed. Although the officially promulgated social justice system permitted me, the Jewess, to work at the University, the feeling of being a second-class citizen remained with me. Nevertheless, I made myself believe that anti-Semitism in Poland would disappear in the future, and the Polish people would become a nation of tolerance.

My opinion about Polish reality changed in the years 1967-69. I watched with disbelief the anti-Semitic campaign organized by the Polish Government and spread by the media.

The few thousand Polish Jews who had survived the Holocaust were publicly accused of treason and described as "the fifth column". Polish authorities intentionally revealed the Jewish origin of those who wanted to conceal it. The Jews were being fired from their jobs en masse and persecuted in many different ways. My Polish friend, terrified by what was happening, offered me a hiding place in her home.

All my hopes for a normal life in Poland failed then. I did not believe any more that Jews would ever be able to exist there without the stigma of their origin. I did not see any future for my son in Poland. The feeling of pre-war humiliation returned and fear reappeared. Disillusioned and embittered, I decided to emigrate. I was leaving behind all my friends and all I had achieved. I was going to an unknown world. The responsibility for my son's and my life lay heavily on my conscience. The tragic history of my life repeated.

In 1971, I immigrated to the United States of America. During the next twenty years I worked as a scientist at New York University in New York, in the field of Biochemistry and Molecular Biology. The long hours spent in the laboratory filled my days. I slowly overcame the difficulties of the English language and became acquainted with American customs and culture. The New World, very different from the one I had lived in, accepted me and it became mine.

I retired from my faculty position at New York University in 1991. Since then I have been living in Sarasota, a small city located on the Gulf of Mexico. Here I decided to write about the time when I ran away from death. I recreated the people and the situations as I have retained them in my memory. They all are authentic. The process of describing the dramatic years of my hiding on the Aryan side was very painful as if I opened scarred wounds. Often I lost hope that I would ever finish my task.

I wrote my memoir in the Polish language in which I felt most comfortable to express myself. My book was published in Poland in 2001. The success of the story of my survival among the Poles was not only a reward for my hardships but also an encouragement for this English translation. It was a difficult and laborious deed. However, the complete work gave me the feeling of the fulfillment of a long due obligation.

My struggle to hide among the native population during the Second World War had a happy ending. Six million European Jews were not so fortunate. Their stories were never written.

Sixty years have elapsed since then. The world changed in so many ways. Unfortunately, hatred toward the Jews remains unconquered, breeding freely in many countries. My story is a reminder of the past and a caution for the future.

Karolina Slowik and her daughters Olga (Dziunia) and Maria (Kamer) were posthumously honored by Holocaust Museum Yad Vashem in Israel the titles of "The Righteous Among the Nations" for saving my life.

587033

Made in the USA

mL

'08